T0207874

The Heart of Awareness for Work/Life Balance

Kris McGuire

BALBOA.
PRESS
A DIVISION OF HAY HOUSE

Balboa Press books may be ordered through booksellers or by contacting:

Balboa Press
A Division of Hay House
1663 Liberty Drive
Bloomington, IN 47403
www.balboapress.com
1 (877) 407-4847

Print information available on the last page.

ISBN: 978-1-9822-3629-8 (sc)
ISBN: 978-1-9822-3630-4 (e)

Balboa Press rev. date: 10/03/2019

Table of Contents

Introduction

Introduction

Happy is healthy!

As we stated before, time and space have their own continuum. Time and space are an illusion to a certain degree. Earth is full of time and less space. The atmosphere above is more space and less time. The balance in life is about putting these two together in a fashion that is beneficial to your life, to your goals. It's about the balance restored to receive more with less. Yes less. Less struggle, less fight, less friction, to gain more with ease.

The goal in life is to get what we want and be successful. Right? And have some abundance of cash along the way to enhance the joys available in life, vacations, extras, etc.

So let's enjoy the ability to get more with less. Awareness is the first step. You must first be aware of your stress, your struggles, and the friction that may surround you.

Secondly, you must believe in an effortless way of doing business. If you are constantly pushing to make something happen then the timing is not right. All should flow with ease. What is blocking you? Step back and be the observer. Is it a person or business plan that is holding back your success? Is it your thought process?

Are you grateful for where you are? Are you grateful for the things that are working as well as those that appear to block you? What could you learn from the block? When you figure that out and are thankful for the block enhancing your learning, you may move forward once again.

Ask for guidance or help along the way. There are many sources and resources of guidance to help smooth out any troubles you may be having. Asking for help is part of the process. Being thankful for the help is even bigger. People, places, and things seem to move and change continuously. Are you able to float? Yes float. That means coast on the wave when necessary. Slow down till the riptide is through and then continue on. While you are floating, take it all in and see what you can learn. What can you learn from the events, changes that have temporarily paused your status in time?

Think about the events and how they affect your bottom line. Now what do you need to change to keep moving along and not be outdated, but to keep up to speed. It will flow flawlessly if you go with the tides of time.

In all things there is a season and then change as seasons do. Be mindful of the normal ups and downs and then they will not get you down. Prepare your mind in advance for change along the way. Simple modifications go a long way towards a fruitful end.

Discovering Your True Purpose

Phases of Learning

Phases of learning are about all of the phases of life we travel through. It's about love and tears, healing and heartache. It's understanding the lives we live and how we live them. In life and in death there is love that conquers "All that is". There is understanding at the golden gates of heaven as to how we lived our life and how it could have been better. There is a new understanding to be carried forward for future growth. An all-out knowingness of what is right and wrong, of what is done in love and what is done out of ego. Life truly is grand and we should live it that way. Enjoying each moment as they come. Feeling the refreshing love of the universe and everything in it. Till next time, live your today's for the tomorrow that never comes.

Distractions – they are all around us all day long at work and at home. So how do we deal with distractions? What can we do to stay focused on the task at hand? Why do we let the distractions in? Is it because we don't really know what we want? Or we don't know what to do with ourselves to move forward? There is some sort of block that is holding you back!

Sometimes these blocks are a good thing. They prevent us from doing something without thinking it through. Other times they are just flat out annoying, but in any case they are there. We will discuss ways to get past them. Ways to let go of what holds you back and open you up to a whole new future with the obstacles and distractions removed.

Let's start by facing the most common obstacle, electronics (TV, phone, iPad, computers, etc.). In the past, depending how far back you want to go or how old you are, some of these objects did not exist. Now they all exist and are for the most part portable. The first part of this step to conquer electronics as obstacles of distraction is to realize what you truly want in life. Do you really want to spend so much of your life on these electronics? Do you know how much time you spend on them? If you limited yourself to one hour of TV a day, one hour on the phone a day, one hour on the computer a day. That is 3 hours of electronics!! Where is your family in all of this? Do you go outside for an hour a day? Do you actually communicate with people, neighbors, friends, or is it all done on the computer via email, or phone via texting. Is your mind numb from the TV shows or so called entertainment.

You must become clear of what you want for your life or nothing changes, including you! If you can't or won't take the time to recognize where you're at in life and what you want out of life, there is no point in going any further in this book. It is about being willing to recognize who you have become and is this who you want to be? What are the distractions in your life and how important are they?

Are your children or family a distraction? I hope not. I hope you do not see it that way. They are your life, which should be your purpose for living and providing. You should be enjoying every ball game, gymnastics class, karate, musical, walk in the park, etc. This should be the joy in your life. If it is not you need to ask why? Why not? What other obstacle needs uncovered or healed so you can fully enjoy life. Because that is what we are talking about in this book, enjoying life and making the most of it.

I use family as an obstacle because it can often feel that way. When you are a mom or dad and constantly running from one event to another, it can be trying on your schedule with work, home, meals, homework, and doctor appointments. Family can also mean caring for parents or siblings. There are many avenues here that need opened up to your conscious mind as to how you feel about them. Once you conquer your feelings and open your perception, things change, balance begins, and with that the happiness rolls in. The appreciation for it all, letting life in and feeling it with life and compassion. Always remembering the blessings we have been given.

People ask for children and everything is fine and dandy the first few years. Then the perception changes from love to work. Children are more work than expected and the word "work" does not have a good connotation, so then love steps aside. Raising kids becomes a job/work, rather than a labor of love. When "love" leaves the picture and life's demands take over, it goes downhill from there and everything seems harder than it needs to be. So we need to bring that "love" and appreciation back into the picture for things to turn around. With a perception of love, you begin enjoying the things you previously viewed as work. Now you can let the abundance into your life because you have changed your vibration to allow rather than reject.

Vibration Awareness Reconciled with Life

So you hear me mention the universe often. Let me explain. We are made up of energy. Energy at its core is a vibration, a frequency. Our spirit/soul is made up of this energy. The universe is part of this energy, this vibrational frequency we communicate on. When our vibrational frequency is in sync or alignment with God, we receive the abundance that resides on that frequency level. So the higher your vibration the greater the abundance to flow to you.

Law of Attraction states, like attracts like. So if you are complaining, you are going to get more of it. If you are loving life and appreciating it, you will get more of it. What do you choose to have more of? More appreciation, more love, more abundance? Or do you choose the lower frequency of energy which pulls you down and continues to spiral downward? I think it is a no brainer, nobody actually chooses the downward spiral. They just don't know how to change it upward. Well appreciation is the upward spiral, being thankful for what you have and those things around you. Continue this appreciation to move upward. As you move up, the universe gives to you accordingly. Keep moving up through the different vibrations/ frequencies and life expands.

Let me put this on a scale for you. The scale is quite large, but in its simplest form 1-10, with 10 being the highest.

1. No desire to exist
2. Unworthy
3. Depression
4. Worry
5. Overwhelmed/Discontent
6. Content
7. Happy with Life
8. Acknowledging Truth
9. Appreciation
10. Love

As you see on this scale there are levels and when you read it, where do you think you are? Where do you want to be? It's a life choice, your Life Choice. What do you want to attract back into your life? Remember the magnet, what energy you put out, you also receive. What is that for you? Remember appreciation at the top. That is the way up the spiral, at any level. From there you realize the love that has been with you all the way, which takes you to the top of the scale. To realize you have been loved and love has been a part of you through it all. You are at the top when you can see the love all around you in all that you do and say and are. Love consumes you and your actions. You are the embodiment of love of God of the universe. You have completed you souls experience and can share with others the true love of God.

So the next time something does not go your way, let it go. When doors shut in your face or do not get responded to in the fashion you expected, let it go. Remember the good that has already taken place. If it is truly meant to be, it will come back around to you. Keep your chin up. Remember you are a strong person, you can do this!

A Fresh Start

Today is a new day. It can be a new adventure for you. Take it one step at a time and see where it leads you. Be cognizant of what feels good and go with it. Learning to listen to your body, your spirit within, is one of the first steps to awareness and beyond. Listen to what feels good. Yes, listen. While listening are your teeth clenched, do you want to knock some sense into someone? (This happens to me often.) Apparently it does not feel good if teeth are clenched. So take time today to just listen and feel your body's reactions. You do not need to take any action. This is solely to awaken you to what is happening around you in your daily environment.

At the end of the day, you can ask yourself "what was the best thing that happened to me today?" Armed with knowledge of what feels good, the best things that happened to you, then you move forward from there. You want more of these things that feel good. It could be specific people, or the work you do, or a town you travel to, or travelling.

What do you see?

Life can throw us some curve balls. It is how we handle them that matters. Do we handle them with love and care? When you bring love back to the core of your being, life flows with ease. No more of the crud or nasty issues. Love is the key to all life issues. It is in learning love that makes life so beautiful, pleasant, and full of joy and happiness.

Where is your love? Let it flow for a better today and a better tomorrow. Love heals all things great and small.

Blessings

In the effort of silence comes forth a great blessing. A blessing to be used for greatness, health, and wealth. A blessing that can by all standards be understood and told/shared between lives. Between the here and now, and beyond. Love is the blessing I am talking about. Love to be shared, past, present, and future. Love of all things great and small. Love of life and the passion within that can create health, and wealth. All of life resides around love.

So what do you love, who do you love, how do you love, when do you love, where do you love? These of course are rhetorical questions to get you thinking about how you share your life. It is shared in every moment of every day, all day long, but do you realize it. Have you ever slowed down to acknowledge how you treat people in every moment? What does that love look like from the outside looking in?

Love is shown in all you do from speaking to someone saying good morning, or a morning hug. To fixing scraped knees and elbows, to lunch with a friend, and of course any personal courtships you may have going on in your life.

It is all around us all day but we often do not see it, or think about it. It is what we do naturally in our way of living. Thinking our way through life as we were taught. Now comes the question of who taught us how to think, to love, to live, to be? We sometimes get lost along the way, from infants to grownups. Infants knew when they came here but all that got shutdown as they grew up. Thinking is influenced by those who took care of us and the influences they had on our lives.

Sometimes this cycle needs interrupted by an outsider to change the perspective on living. The perspective of living within. Seeing things differently. Perhaps through grandparents or another spiritual being.

Who has influenced your life? Good, bad or indifferent does not matter. It is about your openness to be, to accept the truth within. What feels right to you? What sparked that interest? Now what do you do with it once you feel it.

Life and love can be a rollercoaster ride for some, and straight and narrow for others. Some can see beyond and realize there is more than meets the eye. Others choose not to believe, or are afraid to accept the concept that could exist beyond the here and now.

Love is life. Life is love. Our creator is all love, our teacher is all love, and our being is love. I am here to help you get to that place of self-healing, self-love, of compassion for all that is. To help you find your roots deep inside yourself. To awaken your inner being and let your heart do the rest.

The intent of this book is to open the hearts of all that read it for their greatest and highest good. To feel the love flow within your being to know who you really are at the core. The core of life.

I am not going to lie to you and say this is a breeze because it is not. It has been challenging for me as well to get to where I am now, my core within. Each lesson presents its own challenges to overcome in order to move forward. It is the people that have been in my path, each one for a purpose. Some sparking an interest that lead to the opening and the full realization again, of who and what I am. Where will your heart lead you? Who has been an influence on your direction in life? What led you to this point? Something must feel familiar about it to intrigue you. What blessings are you ready to uncover?

Challenges of Love

Christmas time is very confusing to me. I guess because it tests your beliefs. Do you believe is Santa or not? It's not that Santa really matters, more of do you believe in God/Jesus or not? Then do you believe in the bible and how truthful is it?

I find all this upheaval in my heart when I ask these questions. Feeling like something else is missing or is an untruth and here we are celebrating giving gifts to one another. What is it that is missing? Heart!

Yes heart. Are you putting any heart into it? Never mind what you believe or don't believe in Santa/God/Jesus/Christmas, just share gifts from the heart. Do what feels good. So that's part of it, but then some seem to suck the heart out of it by requesting rather than receiving from another graciously. It has turned into a money exchange rather than a heart exchange.

In every gift that is given from the heart, there is a piece of the person that gave it. For instance, my sister's gifts resemble her and her likes. My mom gives the new items they show on TV or in stores for kitchen use. These items are things that she likes but will not buy for herself so gives as gifts.

When you buy for someone, it should be a piece of you with it and let it be. If the other is so reluctant to receive graciously, so be it. Then they are not seeing the light.

That is what has happened to this next generation. Rather than being taught to accept graciously, they whine and complain. Then return items to get what they want, instead of receiving the love they were given. They are then requesting no love in any gifts they are given. Therefore the lack of love is lack of learning lessons in love.

Love is the heart of it all. Literally the Heart of it all. You must master love and the many forms of it to expand/advance your spirit.

Our hearts are full of love to share, for some, it is buried. They struggle to let that love surface to share with others. Sometimes love hurts and can be painful, which is one of the lessons to learn. But also, to let the heart heal the pain and keep trying and sharing. You are helping others more than you know when you share love and feel the pain but keep going. It will get to their soul in the end.

Love may hurt but it is worth it!

Challenges are a part of life, but learning how to conquer them and continue to move forward is the key. I believe I have opened your awareness, I have presented ways to perceive life differently. Now it is up to you to carry forward. It is in your learning and openness to perceive, that will conquer this realm we live in. The beauty that lies beyond is unconceivable in this space and time. The magnificence of it is glorious by no compare.

Enjoy the time while it exists and be free in your heart. The only boundaries in your life are the ones you create. Break free and let your hearts passion flow for the greater good. Let love in and let it flow. It is in time that greatness is revealed.

Life Healing Emotions

Emotions – All emotions come back to love for healing.

1. Hate
2. Anger
3. Judgement

These are the main three to conquer!

Being pure love can be challenging. Work on getting to the root of what bothers you and let love heal the pain. In healing, is peace and knowing.

Follow your emotions – let them lead you. Let them surface. Acknowledge how you feel when they surface. Then ask yourself, why do I have such deep feelings right now? What triggered these emotions? Ask for healing of the underlying cause of the emotion to move forward.

Random or what may appear as random thoughts will come through. Ask what they have to do with the situation/emotion? This is key to healing that instance of it.

Emotions can tell us about our past, lead us in the present, and set the stage for our future.

Learning to deal with emotions as they surface will be the lessons of life to get you to the lesson of love.

The quicker you learn this the better, for a more peaceful, understanding, existence in the current lifetime.

Fear – is an illusion. It is always opposite of the truth.

Herein lies one of the hardest understandings of true life purpose of eternalness. Who am I, what am I, what are we here for, and why?

Fear keeps us in bondage. Slave to being true to ourselves.

Fear is EGO – but that is the nudge we need to understand opposites. Knowing opposites helps us determine what we want vs don't want, or likes vs dislikes. It helps propel us forward to a loving, compassionate being.

Again – follow fear as an Emotion! What is it telling you? Get to the root of the emotion to deal with it and fear will be diminished.

I know I make this sound easy, simple to do, but just sometimes, these roots are very deep and may take time to heal. You need to start somewhere. So pay attention to yourself, your daily grind, recognize what feels good vs uneasy. Then start asking more questions about what exactly makes you feel uneasy, (about a person, a situation, a company, a car) let yourself feel and acknowledge the thought that comes back to you. Your inner self knows, be brave enough to accept it as truth. Then make your next choice accordingly.

Start asking yourself, when given choices, which ones feels better A or B. like going to the eye doctor for glasses, which one is better A or B, 1 or 2.

If neither feels better, then postpone making the choice if possible. If neither feels awful then both are viable choices and either is ok.

It's like going to lunch with friends, 1 – sushi, 2 – burgers. Well if you're allergic to sushi then don't choose 1. But if your choices were chicken vs burgers, and either of these is satisfying, then either is a fine choice. Enjoy your lunch!

Reconciling Fear

So you are probably asking, why do I want to know this or need this? The answer is, in knowing you can change how you respond to fear. What do you believe and is it fear based? When we release fear from our lives we can live with love and compassion for all we do.

Most of our beliefs are based on some sort of fear from childhood. Releasing the fears, the beliefs that no longer hold true, allows your spirit to be freed. It allows your heart to open up and lets love flow.

Victims often feel fear. This is a tough one to overcome I know. There are many forms of feeling like a victim. It is in love of ourselves that we release the fear and victim within to truly live. Once you recognize this feeling and the situation, it is time to do a reality check and ask yourself, what are you afraid of? What is life trying to teach you? Look at it from a different perspective. What are you to learn from this situation and carry forward? Love is opposite of fear. What love can be found in this situation?

Being a victim is typically allowing someone else to have power over you. Why? Why does that other person need power over you? What is that person lacking that they are trying to take from you? Their own self-confidence, and need to empower themselves? But why? Lack of self-love at the core is usually the underlying cause.

So you are wondering, what do I do with this person's lack of loving their self? Life is a mirror. What we see in others that we like and don't like is a reflection of ourselves. You are only victim to another because you allow it and need to love yourself enough to leave the situation.

For most though, they are so deep in, that leaving the situation is complicated. You have given that person your power. Time to take it back. There are services out there that can help with the more severe cases of being victim and getting free.

For those in less severe cases, it is a matter of evaluating your choices. It is time to take a look to see what could be done differently and feel better in your life.

You could feel taken advantage of on a purchase, say a car or home repair, or contractor service of some sort. You always have a choice. Ask for help. Money situations can be as easy as putting it in escrow until the job is done to your satisfaction. The power is still yours and nobody gets hurts or victimized.

The Challenge – Your Puzzle

We have so much to gain when we work together. Each person has a piece of the puzzle. Life is putting the puzzle together. What does your puzzle look like? The roads, the connections, the houses, your work, family, etc., how beautiful is your puzzle. What sections are complete and others that need more work?

How do you find those missing pieces? Are you looking in the right places?

Draw a map on a piece of paper of your life as it would appear on a puzzle. Then fill in the blanks that are not represented. Where does your puzzle lead and end? What do the roads look like, who is on those roads with you? How many houses, how many jobs are on your puzzle map? Do you get to a certain point and you cannot go any further? Draw 2 or 3 roads from there and envision where each will lead you.

Which one of the roads you drew feels better? Any? Hum. Then keep drawing until you find a path that feels good and imagine it real clear supporting you and your family the rest of your days.

How much fun are you having on that road? Any neat vacation spots? Yes put those on too. They are important, places that make you feel good, that intrigue your senses.

Now crinkle it up and toss it. Let life find that road and intrigue you along the way. Feel inspired by events as they happen. Feel the sensations as they surround you. Imagine that puzzle in your mind, smile, and go forward each day knowing you are adding a piece to that puzzle each day of your life!!

Happy travels!!

The Understanding of Why

The reason why!

Why do we do anything? In knowing why, is the answer. It is the driving force. Why meets frustration and peace. Why do you want peace? Because it feels better than frustration.

Trust your feelings to find your Why.

Let your feelings guide you. They will create your why and you move forward from there.

Knowing why is the source of action and not a reaction. You are not responding to an action, you are creating the action.

Picture of Life

Life – until you get frustrated with where you are, you will not try to find or know better.

Frustration meets knowing – you know life is easier, better, smoother, you just have to get frustrated with what you have and LOOK for the knowing in your heart.

Yes there is more to life than work, school, and eventual death.

There are lessons to be learned. We are eternal beings! Think about this Eternal. You are to learn lessons to carry over for eternity, for eternal knowing. These lessons go with you each lifetime. Learn your lessons and keep your eternal being moving forward.

Life lessons are what this dimension is all about!

Each life builds on the last until you master love – being love. Herein is the final lesson.

Love – is final, it is all knowing, it carries all, health, wealth, living, and dead.

Living in love heals all life – past, present, and future.

Once love is learned all other lessons have fallen into place, compassion, trust, caring, hate, anger, disobedience, and obligations. Love is the core for each lesson.

The final lesson is about living in love always!

Keys to Happiness Lead to Success in Life

Let love in.
Share a smile.
Share a hug.
Share compassion.
Enjoy each day, appreciating all the
little things that make it great.
Take time to smell the roses or have a
cup of coffee with a friend.
Enjoy you.
Enjoy being you.
ENJOY!

Appreciation

What is appreciation?

A way of life, a way of living....

Appreciation is constantly recognizing the blessings around you. Appreciation is knowing at all times that you are provided for. Knowing that your needs are always met. It's a state of being.

Appreciating the good moments as well as the bad. Knowing there are lessons to learn and respecting those lessons for what they are.

Appreciation comes in many forms. For instance, the things we take for granted. We begin to expect a roof over our heads, food on our table, a bed to sleep on. We tend to dismiss these items until we don't have them anymore. Then we get mad or upset. Did you show any appreciation for them while you had them?

The vibration of appreciation is right up there with love. It is a high frequency vibration that aligns with the universe to allow everything you have asked for to come to you. It opens doors to a happier healthier you.

People often think it is hard to turn their life around, to get it back on track. When truly, it's not as hard as you may think. It starts by the smallest step of appreciating something around you. It may be a memory, a friend, and an object, a roof over your head, a pillow, or an animal. Start by saying: "I appreciate _____". Keep going through your list. Do this each morning and each night before bed. During the day too if you think about it.

I think you will be amazed at your list for one. Then the changes begin. Doors begin to open, opportunities present themselves, transformation just happens. You begin to carry a different outlook on life and situations. You begin to see things/life more clearly. You may even find your purpose in this life.

Here's what appreciation for your local grocery store might look like:

"I appreciate a place close by, they always have the essentials I need. They are fair priced. I appreciate the companies that make the food that they sell, that the food is available to me. I appreciate the truck drivers that get the food to the supermarkets. I appreciate the fuel makers and gas stations that make the transport possible. I appreciate the truck manufacturers & factory workers that make the trucks and its parts."

This can go on and on. At some point, you will be in awe of the grand life we live and all the luxuries we have. I didn't have to hunt for my food. I didn't have to start a fire to cook the food I hunted. I have a stove, pots, pans, countertop, and food from the grocery store. I am so blessed!! I appreciate the provisions I have in my life.

How do you feel? Better? Life is changing right before your very eyes. Love and God Bless.

Resistance vs Allowing

Resistance

- Know when you are in resistance mode vs. allowing.
- What are your thoughts? How do they feel?
- It's all about feeling the Vibration and knowing where you are on the vibrational scale.

Are you Allowing or Resisting?

Allowing

- Feel relieved or at ease with the situation. No stress.
- Feel at peace with the choices made.
- Ready to move forward to the next step.
- You have a knowing that all is, as it should be.
- See the value in the grand scheme of the situation.

Resisting

- Nothing is working.
- I can't believe they did that.
- That is just so wrong!

- Why does that person always get their way?
- Why in the world is he/she on this project?
- You don't see the "Big Picture".

Awareness = Allowing = Perception Change

- Notice what is going on around you.
- How do you feel about what is happening around you?
- Don't take anything personally.
- Always do the best you can.
- Perception will automatically adjust when you start being more aware and allow vs. resist.

Simple changes can have a major impact on the outcome of reaching your goals & following your inspiration:

1. If the news makes you feel frustrated and annoyed, stop listening to it.
2. Stop watching TV shows that make you feel annoyed or uncomfortable.
3. Be around people that make you feel good, that inspire you.

You want to surround yourself with people who understand your vision and encourage you.

- Who or what are you around every day?
- What do you watch or listen to on the news or radio?
- How do those things make you feel? Happy, good, frustrated, annoyed?
- Identify these influences and make changes to your environment as needed.

What does this have to do with my job?

- Work Relationships

- o   Create synergy.
- o   Build teamwork.
- o   Learn to accept each other's expertise.
- o   Know that everything is exactly as it is supposed to be.

- Workplace Environment
  - o   Know your surroundings and how that affects you.
  - o   Reduce the stress/pressure that surrounds you.
  - o   Meetings and Conference calls.
  - o   Deadlines.

- Feeling the vibrations
  - o   Have you ever walked in on a conversation and felt awkward.
  - o   Have ever walked into a conference room and felt the tension immediately.
  - o   Have you ever thought about someone and then that person called you.

Vibration awareness for work/life balance is about understanding the environment that surrounds. It is in understanding the environment and using it to better yourself. What elements are in the environment that have an impact on you? How do you relate to these elements?

What do you think of when you say the words work/life balance? You think of your job or workplace. Then vacation time or family time and how unbalanced it truly is. So how do you put the two of these together for the greatest good?

Most work places have some sort of plan that they call work life balance. Usually it incorporates time off for family or education, or community events. What they do not have in their work life balance scenario is a reference to vibration or life frequency.

One of my favorite quotes is by Albert Einstein. "Everything in life is vibration."

Life is vibration. Vibrations travel on waves. These waves are long and short, and travel on various frequency levels. Vibrations are also known as energy. So now think of energy flowing on various frequencies.

Thoughts are a vibration. They travel on various frequency levels. The level they travel on is determined by the goodness of the thought. For simplicity sake here, let's take a thought "I love my family." This is a happy, positive thought and good in nature, therefore travels on a higher frequency. Now let's say a bad thought "I hate my life" is riddled with negative connotations, therefore travels on a very low frequency.

Knowing how thoughts travel and how frequency works is part of understanding the elements that surround you daily. If you can imagine a scale of 1-10. Each level is a separate frequency. So let's label these levels to get a better visual understanding. We will say 1 is the lowest feeling negative vibrational frequency and 10 is the highest most positive vibrational frequency.

1. Depressed – Unworthiness – I hate my life, I want to give up and die.
2. Miserable – I dislike everything around me.
3. Overwhelm – I have so much to do, I feel stressed. I feel anxious.
4. Discontent – I am not happy with my life, I know something needs to change.
5. Discord – I feel disconnected and don't know why.
6. Content – I am not looking to change anything.

7. Happy – I feel joy often and okay with my life.
8. Joyful – I laugh and feel wonderful for the most part.
9. Appreciation – I see value in all things great and small.
10. Love – I love my life and everything in it.

These levels are vibrational frequencies that thoughts travel on. When reading through them, did you feel the change in your body recognizing each one. What type of thoughts do you prefer to have? Which level resonated with you? Take time to compare where you are vs where you want to be. This scale is actually much larger. I shrunk it down in my terms for simplified understanding.

If you will notice, I tried to put a feeling with the thought. Feelings are how you identify where you are on the scale. As you become more aware of how you feel, you are able to change it for the better. The goal is to stay as close to 10 – love, as you can. The more often you are above the halfway point (6 – Content), the better off you will be. I will explain this further later on.

I'd like to jump to another very important part of vibrations/frequency/energy. Up to this point I have been using the terms vibration and frequency level. Now let's apply the term energy to vibration. At the core of vibration is energy. Energy acts like a magnet. Now when you look at the scale and ask yourself, how do I feel? Ask what you want to bring back to you! Like attracts like, it is a universal law. Energy is part of this Universe, therefore participates in this law.

So tying these two aspects together. First how do you feel? Do you want more of what you are feeling to come back to you? If you are on the low end of the scale, miserable, I'm sure you do not want more of that. On the higher end of the scale you will reap the abundance of the goodness life has to offer. I'm guessing you certainly would enjoy more abundance of goodness.

Awareness of the Magnet

Your life is like a magnet of sorts. What you do and who you are around determine more of the like. You are a product of your environment. We truly are magnets and bring back to ourselves what we put out.

So think about your surroundings. Are they people, places, things, that you want to continue to be around? Are they satisfying to you? I would love for you to be able to say yes to all of these. But chances are there is something here that may not be satisfying to you.

Your heart is trying to help you identify what needs to change in order to be happy. Listen to your heart. You are asking yourself these questions for a reason. What is the reason? What part are you dis-satisfied with? All of life is about the choices we make daily. Who to be around is a big one. Who makes you feel good? Whose presence inspires you? When you are around people that make you feel good, life is good. Your whole perception feels better.

When you are around someone, and walk away saying "geez I can't stand the complaining, or they have nothing good to say about anything, or geez Louise they are such downers". Wake up call to you, STAY AWAY! This is not a healthy uplifting environment to be in, especially on a regular basis.

Remember we are magnets. Do you want more of that? No you do not!!

We are what we attract. Take a good look at your life and surroundings from an observer point of view. What do you see? Is it filled with laughter and happiness? Or maybe tears, sorrow and pain? Are you the person that is the negative Nellie that others want to get away from. Are you bringing that to you?

Make choices that reflect the life you want vs the one you are blindly following.

You may need to change the company you keep. Friends come and go. The importance of this is to see the value of each friend. It may be to see the value in you. To recognize this specific person could be in your path to help you see what you do not want. Which in turn allows you to choose differently.

Everyone and everything have a purpose to help us on our path. Part of the journey is to see the value, good or bad. Then to enhance our choices. You choose!

Awareness of Emotions and Feelings

Being aware of your emotions and feelings is where all of this begins. When you are aware, you recognize the significance of it. You will recognize when you begin pulling in bad or negative things, situations, or people into your life. Now you can ask for a better feeling to be presented to you. Think of something positive and continue along to raise your vibration to allow the goodness back into your life.

Some get on the downward spiral and cannot seem to pull themselves out. It's not that they can't, they do not know how. It is very easy. Follow a few simple steps and continue whenever you feel you are slipping downward.

1. Take a look around you.
2. Do you see something you can be grateful for?
3. Do you have a roof over your head?
4. Do you have a car?
5. Do you have food in your cabinets?
6. Do you have a job?

It may not be the job you desire, but it pays the bills. You have a roof over your head and food on your table. Your essential needs are met.

Are you grateful for the gas stations that are so plentiful? The makers of the fuel, the truckers that haul it, the makers of the trucks, and the factory workers that make the parts. Think of all the people it takes to make this happen, all the jobs, all the families that are supported along the way. We have many conveniences and many blessings for each one of us if we would only look for them and acknowledge them.

When we acknowledge the greatness that surrounds us daily, we open the doors for allowing the good things of life into our being. Being grateful for the simple conveniences goes a long way towards raising your vibration to the level of appreciation and love. When you are near the top of the scale, you have opened your heart to receive the goodwill of the universe and the abundance therein.

While I understand we have daily struggles in life as well, it is a matter of learning to look at them differently. When you are able to see the lesson to be learned in the struggle, then move forward, is what life truly is about. Those that keep repeating the same struggles, fail to learn the importance of it. They refuse to see the lesson they are to learn. One way to accomplish this is to be the observer. Recognize your struggle or identify it. Now step back and look at the situation from a different point of view, a different angle or perspective.

Usually in stepping back and trying to see the bigger picture outside of yourself, you are able to gain a new understanding of the situation. With the new view you may realize that you are part of a business decision. It is not reflective of you or your performance at all. If you were running the business and had to make certain financial decisions, you may have made the same ones. One of the greatest things to remember is to not take anything personally. When you realize we are all exactly where we are meant to be in each and every moment, life does not seem so stressful. You are able to be the observer of you and others, and not let another's choices affect you. You begin to respect each other more and give them the space they need to learn their lessons as well.

We all have a journey here. Each one is specific to each individual. Yet we need each other to help us learn our lessons together. Someone needs to be the so called "bad guy" in order for another to learn forgiveness and love.

When we accept each other for who we are individually and collectively, we grow in appreciation and love for all that is. We are now able to see ways people, we don't particularly care for, have played a role in our life to help us learn respect, forgiveness, healing, and love.

Within acceptance of "all that is" and knowing we are exactly where we are meant to be, is great comfort and healing in itself. Take a deep breath and let go of the preconceptions and control. Take a deep breath and say "I accept who I am and the choices I have made." Do this 3 times and really feel it let go with each breath. Now breathe in and say "I accept the love and abundance the universe has for me" again 3 times. Now with a grateful heart thank the universe for providing so grandly the conveniences of everyday life and the simple pleasures we enjoy like the water we drink or the air we breathe. Truly feeling grateful for the provisions. Truly feeling grateful for the ability to move forward in life knowing you are loved and provided for in all you do. Respecting the universe and the abundance that surrounds you daily. Are you smiling? You will know when you truly feel grateful in your heart because you will smile and feel good.

Awareness of Joy

Life's joys are found by slowing down the commotion and being in the moment. Enjoy the people you are around. Share their energy, the laughter, and loosen up. Being strict about processes getting done causes stress and pain. Do what you can and let the rest go. What is hard or cumbersome for you is easy to someone else. Pass it off and enjoy the moments, the conversations. Get clear on your direction. What is stressful about getting clear on direction? Not knowing if you are making the right choice! Yes, then wondering if you are getting sidetracked? Just feel it. Whatever feels good, no matter what you may think it looks like or not knowing how it ties in with the journey, just do what feels good. It's that simple for everything in life. Your conversations in the moment, the people, the places, the food, the company, do what you feel inspired to do.

Life Progression

Today I start a new day. It begins here in my journals and continues beyond. I express my being and aptitude in these with the intent to follow through all day, every day.

Life rolls on with or without you. This is something all would do well to accept. Here today, gone tomorrow and the Universe still turns.

Trust in yourself, trust in the angels, trust in the universe. Follow those signs and voices as they appear in your head. They are leading you.

What life brings to the table are ways to show caring for others. When you stop caring and sharing the end is near.

Recapture the life within and share it even if others do not want to hear it. Being productive is part of caring about who and what you are.

Keep moving forward in your workspace or it will pass you by. You may not enjoy or like what you do, but sitting still and not looking ahead will not get you anywhere.

Look at the big picture. How can you contribute to make it a better place?

What can you do to enhance your work environment? Do you like how it looks, how it feels? What are you able to change? Who can you help to ease their load?

When you do your best each and every moment, you can have a clear conscience at the end of the day knowing you did the best of your ability for that day. You are free from the ties that bind you to a sloppy job or one done half way.

Coworkers will notice and soon you are an example for others to follow. This energy carries forward for the entire group. Just simple caring is all it takes.

Personal Growth Established

Who are you?

Who are you? Have you wondered who you really are at heart? Are you a good person with good intentions? Or do you hear what others say and take that to heart? Are you a product of others views or assumptions about you? Or are you something more? A product of the universe, of the energy that surrounds you.

Yes the energy that surrounds you. You are a product of the universe energy that surrounds you. So earlier we talked about how people come and go in our lives. When your energy shifts, the things around you change, to match that energy. The Universal Law of Attraction states that like attracts like. So now is the time to start making choices that feel good and shift that energy to a better place.

As the energy/vibration that you put out changes. The things around you respond to that vibration change. Life is about choices, a series of choices that make up your being. Who you are, what you do, who you have become, and who you want to be, are all a series of choices. You have the power to make it what you want it to be.

By forgiving those in your past, forgiving yourself, you have released that old vibration and can attract something new. You have freed yourself from the confinement of time and space to move forward. What do you want the new you to look like? What do you want to attract into your life? More of the old? Do you want to keep reliving the past over and over? Not likely.

Life in general is a pretty simple feat. It has its ups and downs, laughs and cries, tears and joy, heartache and frustration. These opposites are what make life work. It makes life flow. Without the contrast of likes and dislikes you are lost and do not understand what you truly want. The opposite helps drive you to what you do want. It's like a magnet that repels on one end and connects on the other.

The trick here is not staying in the space of frustration, tears, crying, for any length of time. It's about recognizing the situation for what it is and making a choice to move forward. You must make a choice to change the vibration of where you are. Otherwise you stay in that place and continue to draw those same types of experiences back to you, like a magnet. In order to make effective changes in your life, you need to recognize them for what they are. The situations that arise everyday whether they be family, friends, or work related; how do you feel about them and what are you willing to do about it?

Awareness Awakened

The time has come to move forward in learning. Lessons have been identified. Within each lesson is valuable information for moving forward. The struggles of life are just a means to an end. The end is knowing, the realization of all that is. You know how they say hind sight is 20/20. It is only after you experience an event that you truly gather the meaning of it. These are those life lessons that cannot be read about and understood, they must be experienced. There is no by-passing them or saying "I get it" because you read about it or someone you know experienced it.

There are some lessons that cannot be setup to learn. As in, I give you a step by step to do for you to learn. You just have to flow with life and the lessons will happen naturally. The books you read for learning are to make you aware.

Aware that something has happened and to evaluate it for the lesson within it. Once you become aware, you will realize, looking back at your life, all the lessons you either learned or the scenario that keeps repeating because you haven't learned. There are take aways in every event. Even in the smallest of things like grocery shopping. Were you courteous or rude to anyone? Why? How do you feel? Do you feel good because it was a pleasant experience and you enjoyed the communication? Was it awful? What made it that way?

Take time to evaluate yourself and how you respond to people, nature, events and circumstances. Don't be hard on yourself. Just be aware of your feelings. What drives you, what pushes your buttons? Why do certain things irritate you? Learning to be aware of you, is one of the biggest lessons of life. It is the opening of knowing who you truly are. It allows you to realize what inspires you, what feels good, knowing these things help align you with a future of ease and abundance. Awareness of you is about finding your rhythm of life.

When life flows well, we feel well. When life is jumbled and crabby, you feel awful. Your mindset follows how you feel. So awareness of how you feel sets the tone for your life, your health, your continued circumstances. In a perfect world, how do you want that to look? If you are saying it's not a perfect world, then you have some work to do. Because it truly is a perfect world. There are no mistakes, no coincidences. They are lessons you are not learning and will continue to repeat them until you wake up.

The resources are available if you are willing to ask. You must ask to receive. Once you ask to be open and aware, you will receive the answers to understanding the circumstances that surround you. Remember it is in asking that you receive.

Love Revealed

Love is one of the key factors of life. All of us have loved at some point. Some hearts have been broken by love, while others have expanded by love. In this chapter we will reveal what true love is and how to attain it. If you feel you already know, you may be surprised by the outcome.

Most individuals think of love as a physical love for another individual. But did you ever conceive of love as something more than a feeling? More than "I love you" to someone. Did you ever conceive it could mean love of life, love of nature, love of an act of giving, love of cooking, or love of writing? This love is your passion unfolding. True love of anything has no boundaries.

I'm sure you've heard of "crimes of passion" when someone would harm another to protect their loved one, but let's take another angle on this. Love does not harm anyone or anything. So you must ask yourself what motivates your love. Is it motivated by physical love where one actually Lusts after their partner? Or it is motivated by true love where the hearts are tied together or bound by this other deeper love of self that is shared with their partner?

There are so many variations of so called love, but what does your heart feel? Are you in the relationship because your heart truly feels at peace and harmony? This goes for more than relationships, apply this to your career or job. Do you enjoy it? Does it inspire you? Is your heart guiding you? Or do you not really feel anything? Maybe it's just a job and pays the bills. It could be something you are innately good at but hate. For me that would be computer IT (Information Technology) stuff. I'm good at it, it comes naturally, it pays well, but my heart is not in it. Life is like that you know, full of choices. When my career started I didn't know what I wanted to do with my life. I couldn't hear my heart, it was closed. In the meantime, while trying to figure it all out, I was provided a way to support my family.

Now as my journey has progressed, I hear my heart loud and clear. Hence this book. I want to help others find what is in their heart. I know firsthand how living with a closed heart feels. Now it is open and life feels so much better. So much lighter. Much more laughter. The seriousness is subsiding allowing me to truly live with pleasure.

It is definitely a journey and does not happen overnight. What does happen overnight, is the feeling of being alive again. When your heart opens up or awakens, the sense of wonder like a child is there. You wonder about how things in the universe work, you are intrigued by the concepts of life. All life, animals, bugs, trees, species of trees, and nature. It is so amazing when that hits and you just want to share it with everyone around you. I go into work now and say "did you see that sunrise this morning" or "wow the beautiful colors in the sky last night".

At this point you know your heart is leading and you are truly alive and well. So now it's time to follow your heart and express your true passion. What inspires you? Have you ever been somewhere and it felt so familiar to you but you don't know why? This could be your heart expressing itself to you. Or you meet a person and feel like you've known them forever. Well maybe you have, your heart knows. There is a reason that person has crossed your path. Pay attention, there is a message for you when this happens. It either reminds you of an interest or you have something in common, what is it? Think about it. Life is funny this way, some messages come in the strangest form.

Bottom line, we will explore ways to open your heart, feel what it is telling you. Then offer ideas on ways to progress forward with your newfound knowledge.

Love Acknowledged

Love is kind. Love is strong. Love can bare all things. Love is a key component of living. If one does not love, one does not live. In love is life. Life does not exist without love. Sounds like a riddle I know, but think about it. What drives us each day, each moment? What are we living for? Who or what do we love? Our passion grows with love applied to it. Love extends life. Love heals life. Show love, be love, share love and see miracles come to be.

Miracles are nothing more than love that has come to life. In every miracle, love is at the core. Have you ever heard of those who prayed for healing before surgery and then did not need surgery? Love and miracles go hand in hand. Learn to love freely and see the many miracles you can induce. Feel deep within your heart and let it flow. Love of life, Love of being, Love.

Let's put it all together. We are all one, yet we have alternate backgrounds. Our backgrounds shape who we are and who we become. We have opportunities all around us to see the good, the same in each of us. We can also see the other side of ego and its influence.

Which do you choose to partake in? The ego, individual self where one is better than another, or the wholeness of being one united with all things.

It is a choice we all make all day long. The difference is you. How do you choose to see the world you live in? Do you want boundaries, need boundaries, or do you trust the one of all combined.

These school shootings are frustrated children who need love of all and not shunned by the ego of many individuals in their path. Love is the key. Frustration is letting those around you speak to your ego and not your heart. The heart does not do or say anything that will hurt another. Ego is rough and exuberant, and lacks the power of the heart. Open your heart to see the truth that surrounds you. A hug shared with anyone can heal thoughts, and heal words spoken in ego. Let your heart lead you. Trust in your heart.

To be a saving grace for another, share love, be kind, and be respectful. Let your life revolve around the love you have to share with others.

Trusting others can be a difficult feat when you have been hurt by them. At some point, you need to take control of your actions, your perceptions and put it all in place. Realize people are mostly looking out for themselves and not others. Do not take their actions personally. Rather realize they are in their own world and need not interrupt or influence yours. This realization will go a long way to reeling in your ego and letting your heart lead.

Putting the pieces together and understanding them can take time. Keep an open mind and let your heart tell you what truth is or not.

Love truly is the ultimate healer, be all, do all. Opening your heart, opens the universe to you and everything in it. No boundaries. Love it, respect it, enjoy it, it is yours for the taking with a true heart.

Be kind and loving today! Always one. Thank you!

Awareness of Beliefs

Our beliefs are a huge part of who we are under it all. Beliefs steer your path in life. Part of the journey is understanding what you believe in and why.

Let's say for instance you believe hot water can clean anything and someone else believes you have to have soap. Who is right? Is there a right answer? You choose what to believe and why you believe in a certain way.

Life is just the same. All of your circumstances in life are because you believe one way or another and that directed your path, your way of thinking. We all do not see the same black and white side of an issue. We do not see the same right or wrong in a situation. You must reconcile your beliefs. By this I mean figure out why you believe something is right or wrong as it may be. Then ask yourself where that belief came from. Was it a family belief, a community belief, or your own personal belief? By identifying where you get the belief, you are getting to the core of who you are. Now you can ask yourself do I really believe that or can I let it go.

Let's take medicine as an example. What is your view, does it heal you or not? Some will say yes and others will say no, but why? What influences them one way or another? Either it helped them or it hurt them or someone they love. This is typically what determines your belief in medicine and doctors. Both views are perfectly legit. Now comes the healing. The one who does not believe in medicine will not be healed by medicine. The one who does believe in the medicine is more likely to see results. It's about your thought process, your beliefs. The one that does not believe in medicine would do much better using a natural modality to heal.

This concept is proven in the "placebo effect". A person believes they are taking meds for a specific reason and they get results because they believed in the meds even though it was just a fake pill.

Our beliefs are a stronghold on our lives. It is worthwhile to reconcile your beliefs. Figure out which ones actually serve you for your greatest and highest good vs one that actually hinders your growth in being.

Many struggle with angels, spirits, and eternity. It feels right but then they are afraid to share what they believe in their heart, for fear of being judged by another. The bible mentions angels, people can talk about the bible and their belief there, but bring up angels and it seems to make the topic awkward. Right? Been there, done that!

What most do not realize though is that fear is the opposite of love. Fear can make us judge a topic or situation we are uncomfortable with. In love the same topic is ok for common conversation. This rolls back around to your beliefs. How many times have you heard young children say they saw Jesus or angels? Then the parents dismiss it or think they are imagining it. When in truth children are so pure they do see the angels and Jesus. As they grow up though that belief is shut down by grown-ups.

As we get older it may present itself again and feel totally natural. This is part of reconciling your beliefs. Which one feels more true to you? As you get to the core of your belief system and why one way or another stands out to you. You begin to uncover who you truly are at heart.

Awareness of Heart

The true heart actually resides within your spirit. It is not really a physical part of you at all. It is where your memories reside of all your lifetimes. When your heart hardens, so does your spirit. It becomes less receptive to the energy that surrounds you. Energy is a vibration. There are many levels or frequencies of vibration.

When the heart hardens, it needs something in the environment to spark its memory. The memory of why we are here. The memory of what we are to do with our lives. For most in this hardened state of being, it means being in the presence of this spark that ignites the memories in the spirit. This closeness provides the communication just long enough for the heart to awaken.

Once the heart is awakened, it will continue to unlock the memories within. It will begin to bloom and allow love to manifest within. As this happens, you may see great changes in a person. Starts out as maybe less uptight, or maybe they begin to see things from a different perception. A person may become less radical or less aggressive. The heart begins to own the person rather that the person owning or controlling the heart.

Have you ever talked to a person who has a dream for their life? They are excited to tell you about it. Or the life they live is their dream and they are happy about it.

Then have you asked the college student what are your plans for life, and they shrug their shoulders because they have no clue. No idea where to begin, no dream, no open heart driving them to a passion to fulfill.

These are the obvious differences in an open heart (following your passion) and a closed heart (one that has not bloomed). The goal of this book is for you to identify what type of heart you have. Open or Closed. Then once defined, we will explore ways of opening a closed heart to help it bloom and come alive. If you have an open heart already we will explore ways to advance it to the next level and what that means to you.

This will be a journey of self-exploration. A journey of self-reflection and identification. You will be amazed at the power of your heart. Not only the physical power to pump blood to keep your body moving and alive, but the power to conceive of a life of no boundaries.

The burdens of daily life can weigh us down. It drains our energy. When you are enthused about what you are doing, you are not tired or drained. You are happy and carefree, enjoying life rather than dreading getting up for work each day.

Your life can resemble your dream or it can resemble your nightmare. So I ask you which you prefer. I am absolutely positive you prefer the dream. So now I ask, "do you focus on the dream or the daily struggles of life? I am betting most will say the struggles because they affect your daily life the most. Yes? So here is the clincher, what we focus on is what we get more of!! What we focus on, we get more of!! Awful right? Well only awful if we focus on the struggles. Great if we focus on the dream and are inspired.

This is energy and vibration that our body, AKA "Our Heart" responds to. Energy is the key. So I will help you understand how energy/vibration plays a huge role in our lives. When you understand this and live within the context of energy. You can maintain a high level vibration. You change what you bring into your life. Your struggles can be over and a new chapter of your life begins.

Life is a journey but it has many variables. It is perceived differently by all. One may believe it's about money or status, another may believe family and relationships are what life is about. Your heart is what determines the perception you choose to view it from.

Your heart is the key to living. If your heart stops, the rest of you stops, right? So your heart should be the focal point of all that you do. An open heart has love for all things. It sees no boundaries, it loves unconditionally. The heart perceives life. The heart can also be your biggest barrier. A closed heart gets coarse and refuses to let love in. Love heals even the coarsest of hearts. A pure heart is in a child. They are born into this world and have no preconception, no barrier. A child loves all. A child's heart is open.

As time goes by children learn from the environment around them. It either keeps their heart open to perceive life, or it begins to harden and get coarse over time.

Awareness of Judgement

In the end, we are a product of what we believe and how we let it guide our lives. It all starts as the truth but somewhere down the line we forget to keep asking for the truth to show. We start to make our own. What is my truth? Love to be loved, share love to all kinds not just the kind. What good is it to share and show love to the kind only. Be love and share love to all those in need and those not in need.

Love heals all things, good, bad, evil, indifferent. Just be love. Sounds easy but sometimes it's hard to love or show love to someone whom we may have passed judgment on. Why are we judging? From within we feel threatened. What is the threat? A fear you have not faced so you judge another to pass it from you.

Judgement is God's mirror of yourself. He puts the mirror in front of you whenever you need it most. Just so happens, most of us do not realize we are looking in the mirror at ourselves.

Awareness of Self

Aspects of life come at us from all directions. From friends, acquaintances, loved ones/family, to the author of a book. With so many influences, one has to ask themselves, which one is right? There are lots of opinions in the world. The answer to that is within you. What feels right to you? Your heart knows what it needs and wants. It will guide you to the information that is right for you.

It's like when you meet a stranger yet feel like you have known this person forever. That is how the information will feel to you. It will feel like truth and your heart resonates with it. It is the missing puzzle piece that makes the picture whole. Life truly can be looked at as one great big puzzle and you are putting the pieces in place to complete the picture. When you see the whole picture it all makes sense.

Some people do not enjoy putting puzzles together because they do not see progress fast enough. They want to see the completed puzzle in a short amount of time. These same people can react to life the same way. They want it to move forward but are not taking the time to enjoy the journey along the way. This journey is experiencing the different pieces of the puzzle.

Then putting them together to make sense of your journey, your purpose.

As I stated earlier, our purpose is very simple. Just "Love". Love life, love people, love nature, love of all that is, unconditional love. I know it sounds redundant and boring, but so many aspects of being are just about love. When you get to the core, trust in it, trust your heart to lead you.

Our journey is meant to bring out the best in us. That which is for the greater good. Our journey is meant to learn compassion along the way. Learn unconditional love. See the beauty in all aspects of life/nature. Our journey is in slowing down to take in what is around you. Smell the roses or coffee as it may be. See the colors, feel the textures, hear the sounds of the smallest cricket to the airplanes in the sky.

Enjoy the wonder and amazement of the life that you have set forth here and in the past. How you lived, and helped create the here and now. Is life full of chaos and turmoil or love and delight? Where do you want to be in the mix of it all? We have choices to make every day. How do you want to choose to live? Enjoying what is in front of you or counting down the years to the end. I suggest finding your passion and choosing to live in enjoyment.

Awareness Roadmap

When you are able to take a step back and look at all of life as an observer. You begin to see it differently. Take for instance, all of life is like a board game.

Imagine taking a road map and putting it on the table in front of you. Look at where you live, the path you travel to work, to school, to the doctor, the dentist, restaurants, and entertainment.

Now imagine your neighbor's path to the same things, his job, his doctor, his dentist, and entertainment. It is different than yours right?

Each of us are on our own path of life. Our own game board with our own goals to accomplish. We each make choices according to the needs we want fulfilled. Where do you feel your life is lacking? What needs could be filled to satisfy that void. Eventually you will figure out what you are lacking and be able to fill the voids on your own road map of life.

Follow your heart, follow the inspiration within you. This is the key to filling the voids you may feel in your life. It may lead you on a path of healing and forgiveness of yourself. Don't be hard on yourself when you realize some of the choices have been a lifetime in the making and take time to turnaround. Be gentle and loving with yourself and remember everything always turns out for the best.

Be willing to accept the perceived mistakes and acknowledge them for the lesson you have now learned. It is another step forward on your path. But this time it is a conscious step forward and not one of following. Be proud of yourself and these realizations as they come. These are real truths being given to you for your benefit. Now that you have recognized them in your life, you have made a huge step forward in your understanding, of why you are where you are, and can continue to make progress.

Release Yourself to Love

What other beliefs are holding back healing. Judgement. Judgement of why you need healing in the first place. Judgement comes in all forms. From lack of self-esteem, to an overactive ego, and everything in between. So we'll use our body for a simple example of how this works.

How forgiving is your body for the abuse you put it through?

Does your body view it as abuse or do you? Release judgement. Your body just is. It does not hold grudges. It is you preventing the healing for not forgiving yourself for whatever incident caused an injury to your body. Forgive yourself, love yourself.

Your body is just a tool at your command to get you from one place to another. You can do whatever you want and mishaps along the way can be healed. Heal yourself with love and forgiveness.

Let love in. Release judgment and feel good about who and what you are.

Recognizing and Acknowledging

Awareness of Work/ Life Balance

By now you are probably wondering, what learning about the energy, vibration, and frequency has to do with my job? The balance is in knowing who you are and what you want out of this life. To find true balance you must be content in work and home.

Learning your purpose
– God's Will for you

How many of you read the bible daily?

Maybe 10 or 15 minutes each morning or night before bed. So I am going to ask you to journal for 10-15 minutes each day. Preferably when you have peace and quiet.

Start out with prayer to God/Source thanking him for your many blessings. Or even just for a beautiful morning, or sunset and ask for guidance as you write in your journal. You can just start writing or ask questions and pause for a moment to hear the answer. Often your question is answered as you are writing it. Before you are done asking it is answered. Write down what comes to you no matter what it is. It may be a word or phrase, just write it down. It will make sense later.

God's voice sounds like your own. So when you are having thoughts and sometimes talking to yourself. That voice you hear is the same voice of God. So don't expect it to be like the movies where it is some other loud voice. It is very subtle and sounds like your own voice.

If you don't get an answer or don't recognize it right away, "No Worries"! It'll come, be patient. Some questions do not get answered right away. Go on to another question or write what is on your mind. Sometimes what is on your mind is your answer!

When I go back and reread my journals, I'm amazed at the answers that are written and I didn't see it at the time. God/ Source always answers, we just don't want to always accept the answer given.

Sometimes we have a hard time with the receiving part. There are times we will receive immediately and know it. There are other times we don't think God/Source gave us an answer, but the true answer is really in <u>not</u> receiving what we asked for. It may be that what we asked for is not for our greatest and highest good. Other times we need to wait and be patient to receive.

There are times when our thoughts block ourselves from receiving. Because we are focused on the receiving for the wrong reasons (greed, hate, mischief, etc.). The trick is to focus on <u>why</u> you asked for something. How will it make you feel to get what you asked for? Now you are not focused on receiving but feeling happy about your intentions. This process opens the allowing of what you asked to come to you. If you are focused on the outcome you may be blocking it from coming to you.

Angels & Guides in the Universe work for Source to provide for you according to his will for your life. We all have a specific purpose here. Some are different than others. We are to ask for help and divine guidance from these beings.

Our lessons to learn here vary as well. We are all here to help each other learn our lessons. This is where service to others comes into play. We cannot make someone understand or do it for them, but we can be there to encourage them. We can console them and help them through a rough spot. We are here to lean on each other for understanding, to grow as individuals, and to become one with God/Source.

We are all one in God and we have different spiritual gifts as provided by God. Point is, we all have our specialty/skills in life. Are we using them to the best of our ability, for our greatest and highest good? Some of us are already where God/Source wants us to be. Others need to be opened up to God's will for their life.

In the end, we are all eternal beings. We all die an earthly death, but that is not the end. Life continues. Where will yours lead you?

If you can master God's/Source will for you in this life, so it will be in heaven as well. This is where Heaven on Earth meets the road. You can make Heaven here on Earth or you can make it Hell on Earth. It's your choice. I prefer Heaven myself.

Timing Recognized

I am realizing tonight that I push instead of waiting on the timing of the universe. I realize how discontent it makes me feel to wait and not know what to do with myself in the meantime. I need a hobby. I feel most content when I am physically doing or physically engaged in something.

Love Healed – Love Conquered

Let us see all the ways we love. We love our children, our spouse, our family, our home, our car, our space, our job, our neighbor, our friends, our animals, our plants, our trees, our sunshine, our snow, our environment, and last but certainly not least ourselves.

Take a few moments to look around you. Take a walk and absorb all of the things you love. Take time to smell the roses or coffee as it may be, but enjoy something around you that brings a smile to your face. Now remember that feeling and capture more of those moments in each day. Pretty soon you will be smiling all the time.

Love heals in mystical ways. Try to see and feel the love around you. Let it in to your being. Now enjoy the beauty of it. So simple yet so essential to being happy.

Example of a
Gratitude Journal

I enjoy the flow of a good pen. I enjoy the intriguing thoughts. I can put them on paper.

I am very grateful for my path. I am hopeful it will continue to grow. I can see so many ways to apply joy in my work. I know the universe is working for me and I should not push it. It will come naturally and proceed from there when the time is right.

My only job is to be me and stay in tune with the energy. Stay intrigued with life and the possibilities that will follow. It will be a completely smooth and seamless process. Trust the universe is aligning the elements for you. Just be you. Simple.

I would love to stay tapped into the healing energy of the universe love. Please save me from myself and let your pleasures be. Thank you for your care. Thank you for your desire. Thank you for a human well kept. Thank you for love gone wrong. Thank you for love gone right. Thank you for this day, that I may see the light. Thank you for your heavenly hosts. Thank you for there will within. Thank you, my love abounds. My joys, my loves, are yours to be found. For this me is ending and a new one begins.

Keep today in the moment and never rescind. Be here be strong for one will waver and one be strong.

Let the will of time take its toll. You are well and that of old. Be you, be me, we be together till the end. Wake up inside, feel the pleasure of when.

Your love is true we know it is. Feel your love and go be you! Thank you. Thank you. Thank you.

Awareness Revealed

It's true our lives are a reflection of how we feel about ourselves. We see in others what we choose to see. We see the reflection of our self, good or bad. The good or the bad is your choice. What or which do you choose to see?

Bottom line, if you do not like what you see in the mirror, you reflect that all around you. You will see pieces of you in others and pick it out and criticize it.

On the flip side, when you look in the mirror and feel good about yourself, that is the reflection you see in others. The pleasing aspects of you, the things that feel good.

When you realize your reflection in your surroundings, it is a sign of the direction your life is headed. If things are going good keep at it. If things seem to pile up and complaining a lot, move on, address the real issue inside you not others, and keep moving.

Release Prayer

Lord God above, I ask for assistance in helping me let go to let in. The human part of me really wants this but my heart is on the edge. I ask my heart to open to the goodness the universe has to offer and ignore the rest. Be the light within and let go, let in and shine on! Thank you. Thank you. Thank you!

Awareness of Claiming the Power

⚬⚬⚬

You know, it's funny how we go through so much of this life following. Thinking we are following our path of life, never actually realizing, we are creating this path, not following it.

Follow takes no conscious intent. Creating does. Or does it? It all happens whether we realize it or not. A marvelous thing for some and others, not so much.

Let me explain. When you think you are following through on your life and just take it day by day, you tend to get bored but keep going anyway. Eventually you question; there must be something more to life than this? Right!

As you question, learn, and open up to other possibilities, you begin to realize, you created this life by the choices you have made. If you are bored of your hum drum daily life, remember, you created it and you can change it.

The power is yours. Choose differently.

Let's take another look at following your life path, vs. consciously creating your life path. Make conscious choices to have a direct impact on your path.

Take your job for instance. How did you get it? Why did you choose it? Is it something you are passionate about?

I can tell you most of the world is in a job for money to pay the bills. They are not in the job because it is something they truly love doing. Many jobs are just a stepping stone to the next phase of life. It may be to get you through college, to provide some spending money. Or even a job you are good at but don't really like. Somewhere down the line you acquired a skillset that has enhanced you to provide a substantial income for daily life.

Is that skillset something you are passionate about? Does it still intrigue you? In other words has it still captivated your interest to keep doing?

For some it may be an innate skill but not one that you are passionate about anymore. It has served you well but maybe it's time to move on. What are some other interests? What do you find yourself thinking about? Are you wanting more? Wondering about more to life? Just maybe the job and career are fine and you are perfectly content. Yes.

Could it be you are questioning life in general; your purpose, your family, your beliefs and religion. Are you feeling some kind of tugging at you that there is more to be revealed but kind of scared to find out what it is?

It's okay to have these thoughts and explore what's behind these doors. It is a craving that your inner self is trying to get you to see. This is part of the magic of creating your life rather than blindly following a path.

It's an inner awakening of your soul's expression to this life you lead. It is a yearning to express the creative power within!

Awareness of Eternity

The humility of life and its adventures are the stories of time. People need to know history in a two-fold fashion.

One is the history of their soul and what it has been through for growth and learning. The other is the physical history of time and its influences of earthly events and how they have affected the environment you live in daily.

Much to discover. Books have come a long way to retain history. But we all see history from a different perspective. What is right, fair, or truthful? All of it? None of it? You have to decide and choose what to believe.

The beliefs ingrained in your eternal soul or the beliefs of one earthly generation to another? It's time to do some exploring to find out who you really are under it all and release the "you" within. Then you can begin to make sense of the environment around you.

Where to begin? Let's start by clearing the memories of far and beyond that do not enhance your journey of this day and age.

First step, you may be afraid of clearing something of the past because you learned it for a reason. Yes. But your soul now knows its purpose has been used and time to pass it by. So now you are wondering what exactly is this and how do I do it, right? Next step is to release the conflict within your heart. The conflict of right and wrong. Right and wrong in general. There is never a right way or wrong way of doing or being. Each is specific to each individual.

There is no perfect or perfection to be had. Healing is done in many ways, many forms, no right or wrong way to heal a person.

Here is a release exercise to get you in motion:

I release in me the need for perfection and correctness. I release the views of a right vs wrong aspect of being and doing. I allow in the divine guidance of God and the universe to my being for its greatest and highest good. I ask to receive the release of this perfection I hold within for my greatest good. I ask for the allowing of God's divine purpose into me for my greatest good. I ask to receive this allowing and the divine abundance of love and healing of my heart that comes with it. Thank you. Thank you. Thank you. I am deeply grateful and appreciative for the love and support. Thank you.

Life Recognized

Turn the page, the new page of your being revealed in love and light. Take a step back in time and remember the life. The life of you, your spirit, no boundaries. Life just floated, no worries, no cares, and no responsibility. All you did was "just be", "Just BE" that's it, simple. No thoughts to battle, no right or wrong bouncing back and forth. It was so simple to "Be".

The earthly space changes things a bit. Viewed differently, perspectives, right vs. wrong, good vs. bad, you know the game all too well. Each scenario as it plays out and unfolds. Where is the beginning? Where is the end? That is the human earthly dilemma. Not to know or be known by any one being. Life is a mystery not to be taken lightly. (HA made a funny "not to be taken lightly"). We are light and light has no beginning or end. Light shines and is always, never faltering or giving way. Light is light as in "light weight". Humans are heavy and yet have a hard time being light! It's an illusion to be understood. To know light and be light in its many forms.

Resolution Recognized

First step is to identify by opening your awareness of what is around you. Second step is then in knowing what you like versus what doesn't feel so good. Third step will be to strive for more of what feels good. Bring more of the goodness into your life. Fourth step will be to live happily ever after.

Navigation

Releasing the Ties That Bind

The ties that bind can be strong but they can be broken. Asking is the first step to every movement. I ask for my journey to begin. I ask for enlightenment to encompass me. I ask for love to consume me. I ask for love, hope, joy to be a part of me. I ask for all things to flow in and through me with love at the core and the light to shine. I ask for freedom to be me. I ask all of this in the love and light of the universe. Thank you.

I ask for guidance raising my children. I ask for guidance supporting my friends. I ask for guidance for my relationships. I ask for love to be revealed. I ask my heart and higher self to reveal themselves for my greatest and highest good. I ask for fear to subside and let my heart lead. I am grateful and thankful for this journey.

Conquering Overwhelm

You are recovering from an overwhelming weekend and just need some time to decompress and get back on track. You do not have to have full passion/drive every day to make it. Taking time for yourself is very important. Otherwise you get burnt out and feel stressed.

Most importantly: set realistic time aside for you, as well as dedicated family time, and of course time for work. It will all come together. Just let it flow.

Thank you for allowing the time needed for every aspect of my life. Thank you for the release.

Recognizing the Illusion of Time

Time is an illusion. Yet one we rely on so boldly. We think time controls this life and everything in it. We associate some sort of time to everything we do; Age, Birthdays, Dates, Clocks, Calendars, the list goes on.

The only truth to live by and does not have a time attached, is how you treat people. Are you loving, compassionate, forgiving? Do you share and help another or hoard for your own being? Are you willing to help another? How much love do you share with those you meet? Do you hold grudges?

The true test of time is how well you used it for the greater good. Grow your heart, grow your spirit. Some of us have completed these lessons already and are here to share and help others on their path to eternal knowing. Are you willing to accept the truth of life? Is there more to uncover from within me, to expose, or clear?

Mirror – Judgement

Mirror – reflection of yourself in others.

What do you see?
Why do you feel you have the right to judge others?
Are you judging them or the action?

Judgement is seen in many ways: racism, favoritism, housing, clothing, speech, type of work, etc.

Workplace: job level, clothing, type of job, pay, worthiness, vehicle, etc.

So what part of yourself are you dissatisfied with? Your own dissatisfaction is what causes you to judge others. When you finally accept yourself as you are, then you no longer judge others.

You must learn to accept yourself. In acceptance is love. Then you love yourself for who you are.

Soon love appears in all forms and you need not judge anymore but share love with all. When you look in the mirror you see love and acceptance of all that is.

Influence of Vibration

Taking a few seconds to read the energy/vibration that surrounds you can have a major impact on your outcome of life. When you feel the vibration is uneasy, you will know how to change it. By changing it for the better, you have increased the abundance around you.

Keeping yourself in higher, better feeling atmosphere plays a major role in your life outcome. Wouldn't you rather be in a pleasant atmosphere vs a depressed complaining one? Continuing in that depressed surrounding wears on you and will bring your energy down. You will feel tired and exhausted. Staying in this actually begins to affect your health and well-being. So in recognizing your vibration, you can change it. Change it for you, for your health and well-being.

These simple changes can be a quick fix to an immediate situation; go for a walk or just walk away from the current surroundings, take a deep breath, relax, and re-evaluate how you are feeling. How temporary is the situation, a few minutes, or a few hours. Walk away, go to the restroom, find a way to give your body and mind an escape. Even if only for a few minutes, it is better than not collecting yourself to come back to whatever situation with a new frame of mind. You will feel refreshed and ready to take on another round of exposure to this low vibration.

Ultimately, you want to eliminate these lower vibrations from your surroundings as much as possible. This will improve your health and well-being. It will allow the abundance of the higher frequencies to come into your presence. More contentment, love, passion for being and doing for you.

Stability Recognized

Get to that place. The place of peace and suffering.
Peace and suffering are one and the
same. You suffer to have peace.
You have peace only after you have suffered.
You must get low enough to suffer to know how peace feels.
Frustration and know how are one and the same. You must
get frustrated enough to want to know how to do something.
Opposites – you need one to know the other!!
This is life.

Recognizing Discontent

Many choose to be bored. They choose boredom because they cannot feel their heart. One must awaken their heart to feel alive. An open, awakened heart has the ability to give direction. Direction to living, to being, to doing, to follow a passion within.

When you find you are bored or do not know what to do with yourself, sit quietly for a moment. Then ask your heart what it desires to do next. Let the thoughts flow and choose one to act on. Your heart does not just choose one thing. It will give you options, like go for a walk, read a book, get outside, or relax with a movie. For each is different, and the options will all be suitable for you. Sit quietly for just a few minutes and focus on your breathing. Count in 1, 2, 3, 4, 5 and out 1, 2, 3, 4, 5 and in 1, 2, 3, 4, 5 and out 1, 2, 3, 4, 5. Breathe In, Breathe Out, In and Out. Feel your chest in and out. Now ask what next? Listen to your thoughts.

It really is quite simple. If you are parent, chances are you won't get finished with the in/out and you will be interrupted with your answer to "what next". It will be right next to you, or a phone call. Trust me, the world works in mysterious ways.

If you are truly that bored, take a nap and re-energize your being. Could be you just need time to recuperate.

Implementing in the Workplace

Vibration awareness in the workplace is about being willing to feel what works and what does not.

Know which avenue to take and when. Not fighting the flow but going with it.

Making valid changes along the way for a better tomorrow. Most people resist change because it has been pushed on them and does not feel natural or beneficial.

Most changes are pushed from the top down by executives that are not in your work environment.

Synergy is about working together to find the best solution for all parties and then implement it.

Having a voice in the outcome is a big deal. It means someone has the opportunity to speak up and share what's important, so the best solution can be recognized. Then thought through for a potential implementation.

Implementing from the top down seldom works and another one will be pushed when they realize the last one was ineffective.

So the ball rolls. Who is willing to be a voice and feel the energy, the synergy needed to make valid changes for the benefit of everyone?

How do you get your voice heard and what do you do when they are willing to listen?

Do you have a plan? Ask the right questions and it all falls into place.

What are the right questions; who is in control, who are the decision makers, and what is the big picture behind it all?

Answer these questions and then you can formulate a solution that benefits all parties involved.

Vibration awareness is also knowing you are on the bottom of the totem pole and have little say in the happenings.

The best you can do is keep your team working together for the best outcome of each and everyone involved.

Create a workplace where people understand each other and can get along. Then they see the same big picture goal for the team and can work towards it together.

Being a voice is not always an easy job. Many will hear you but not listen. Synergy is using vibration awareness to get each on the same page.

When that happens, you can move mountains.

Find what works and replicate it. Are any of the groups working well together? Are they all scattered and not really in sync with one another?

What does it take to get them on the same page? A meeting in person, not video. In person the energies can mesh. This way they feel it and can air out any concerns to move forward.

When all is in sync, you will have smooth sailing. It won't happen without help of management to support the effort.

Keep trying. Do not lose faith. You may be surprised by the responses. It just may get where it needs to be!!

The journey is not about careers or status, it truly is about the heart. Unlocking the memories of your past and pulling it all together for a better brighter future. A life of love, sharing and happiness.

Remembering can be a challenge. It will happen mostly in dreams. You may not remember the dream but your heart remembers and can carry that forward. Our lives are about a past, how to make it right, how to grow, then in moving forward.

Recognizing Patterns

We all have patterns. We do things a certain way over and over. We tend to see things the same, over and over. How often have you looked at the same tree in your yard and not given it a second thought? You see it, but do you SEE it? Our patterns of life are the same way. We just do them, go to work, go to dinner, go to a game, but do you really see what is around you? Do you ever stop to wonder, like a child? Do you ever get curious about how nature works, about how we as a human function? Our pristine bodies and how they function with no intervention. They just work.

We like to follow patterns because a pattern is like a recipe. It is laid out a certain way and if we find a path within that works, we follow it.

Take a moment and think about a quilt. Its pattern is often random yet precise. In order to see the beauty of it, you need to take a step back to see the whole thing. The beauty isn't in one square or triangle, it is the combined pieces that create the beauty put together in a precise pattern. Hence is life. Sometimes you need to step back to see your pattern and appreciate the full beauty of where you are and where you are headed.

We develop patterns of living, patterns of values, patterns in morals, patterns in raising our families. I ask you for a moment to step back and see the value of it. Is there a piece of the pattern missing that could be changed to complete the quilt?

Are there people you need to forgive, situations that need forgiven. Forgiveness is a big piece to completing our pattern. Teaching our children to forgive is often one piece of our pattern of living that is left out. Children are taught forgiveness by receiving forgiveness and love. It has to be part of the life style. Forgiving others or situations that happen and not let it block your progress going forward.

As adults, we tend to follow the patterns of our parents. Take the view of the observer and see those patterns clearly. Do you want them or not? Make choices, make patterns, make beliefs worth living by. Be the observer from the outside in, to see what patterns you live by.

Splendor Recognized

Put on paper all the glorious, wondrous things the Universe/ Source/Creator has put here for us. For our pleasure. Write about each one in detail. See the glory of everything in your life and around you; nature, kids, family, animals, trees, seasons, holidays, baking, cooking, and even laundry.

Every component of my life that has brought me to who I am and why I am here.

The splendor I see!! Do you?

I was reminded tonight of all the wonderful things that are before us to be grateful for. Who knew how gratifying doing laundry could be? The constant up and down, movement all day. Switching loads, folding, putting away, starting another load, keep the cycles going. It keeps your body and mind occupied. How glorious is that!

Splendor is not always in what we can see but rather what we can do. Some is seen, some is not. Follow your heart to find the true splendor within. It is not seen but felt. How do you feel, is a very real, yet illusional perception.

Feel great, be great
Feel happy, be happy
Feel love, be love

Feel yourself expand to the depths of the earth and to the sky above. Feel the expanse, be the expanse. It is all within you. Not seen from the outside looking in but inside out.

Be like the tree and the roots.
For as it is above, it is below!!

Recognizing Disconnection

Why today do I feel the way I do? This discontented, disconnected, no drive, feeling? I am aware of a need for comfort, to be comforted. I am feeling disconnected, and discontented. Focus and you will find what you are needing inside of you at your core. Let your love shine.

Be honest with yourself!! What do you want to live for? What is at your core? Let go of all the commotion and feel the love deep inside. We are energetic beings of light, all of us, all connected whether we believe it or not. "It Is".

Be true to your heart, let your dreams flow, no control.

Release control, release the pain, cry the tears, and regain your life.

Learn to let go in order to live more fully.

Family struggles, relationships, hardships. Recognize, to release and come to a better place in life.

Freedom is a feature of living within certain boundaries but outside of others. Freedom to be you and enjoying the life therein.

Relax in the Outcome

Influence of Time

Time is our portal to all that is. Time is an illusion but at the same time it is a constant for our lives. We revolve around time. Everything we do consists of time of some sort or another. It may be a date/day, an hour, or even measured as a lifeline.

Time in the past had no meaning. Seasons, the sun and the moon, provided a sense of time for measuring the harvest, so called timeline. When to plant and when to pick. So this became the beginning of "time" as a unit of measure, but not the "beginning of time".

When you stop to contemplate all the references we make to time on a daily basis, is pretty incredible. We allow time to dictate our lives. What time to get up, when to be at work, what shift we work. When to eat, when to take a break, work schedule, school schedule, classes, and meetings. Vacation time and how much of it. How much time off work to spend with family. Businesses run on time, what hours they are open or closed. Holidays, birthdays, age, and the like, you get the point! Our paychecks are based on time.

So what does time offer us and why is it so important to us. If you did not have to conform to time, what would your life look like? Try for a day to not reference time. Pretty weird isn't it. You know just by thinking about it, how many times in a day you reference it. We almost don't know what to do with ourselves without time dictating the next step.

Let's take a moment and think about your life and what it would look like if time were of no consequence. Where would you be, what would you be doing? Does it change the enjoyment level in your life? Does it change your occupation? Does it change how young or old you feel? Does it change where you live?

I think if you really thought about it. You may not have the same occupation, or live where you live. Some like to live close to work, so less traffic and travel time. Would your occupation change if time to clock in/out did not exist and pay was not a reflective of hours worked. Would you find your passion and let it consume you? Doing something you love with no reference to time.

Ultimately our lives would change a great deal without any reference to time. Where do you want your life to be? Where do you want to be? Take some time to ponder these thoughts. Yes "time" to ponder "time" and its influence on you and your well-being.

Why does our existence need quantified by time? A beginning and an end, when as a spirit you are eternal and time is an illusion.

Natures Marvels

The science of vibration is in interpreting the frequency. The frequency of the vibration, heals on different levels.

Each gemstone is a unique frequency, therefore heals only on that frequency. Learn the frequencies and then align the healing needed with the proper frequency.

Some frequencies are mental and others are felt on the physical level. Let your body lead you to the needed frequency for your healing.

Plants have vibrations also. All of nature is vibration, earth energy. What does this have to do with you? Being in nature, surrounded by natural earth elements can raise your vibration. Go for a walk, sit at the park, and absorb the natural earth energy that surrounds you.

Being in nature is the easiest most natural way to raise your vibration, clear your head, body and soul. Relax in it. Remember that old saying "take time to smell the roses". Well just that, slow down enough to take time for yourself. Enjoy what is around you.

Awareness of Work/ Life Balance

Work life balance can be tricky. It's partially about dedication. Learning to distinguish when to be dedicated to work and when to be dedicated to family or self.

If you look at one of those old fashioned gold weighing scales, they measured by the weight put on the tray. Imagine taking a marble for every hour and placing it on the tray, one side for work the other for home. What would it look like? Is it lopsided or semi-even?

When you are home or have a home business, do the same analogy. A marble for each hour you spend working vs. the hours you spend for yourself or family. How balanced is your scale?

Most will find their scales are truly unbalanced. They will see how much time they dedicate to work or community and less to themselves.

Another way to look at the scale. Measure it by putting a marble on the scale for what you enjoy vs. feel you have to do.

This type of measurement is much more accurate for your well-being. I have talked about feelings. What feels good vs. what does not? When you feel good you are promoting health and wellness. When you do not feel good about what you are doing, you tend to get run down and illness can set in.

Many people enjoy their jobs or the work they do. Whether it be volunteering, or working for someone else, or being self-employed. So now when you do the marble on the scale you may find it to be much more balanced. Or not, if you are not allowing time for a home life, for yourself. Only you can make this designation. You are the one in need of balance. This is only one way of looking at it, only one of the many ways to measure it.

If you are happy with your life style, then you would not be reading this book. Contentment is a big deal in the overall scheme of life. When you are content with what you have and appreciate it, you are promoting health and wellness.

Many times in relationships, one will be totally content while the other is yearning for more. Wanting to know what else has life got to offer. They have this internal knowing that there is more and are trying to find it without disrupting what they already have.

This is a personal balance that is seemingly hard to attain. Life will bring it to you. But are you willing to make choices to upset the current to have long term health and wellness within? The search has begun within your heart when you feel this way. Let your heart lead you.

Health and wellness are important. We come across many circumstances when one is fighting for their human life due to illness of one sort or another. The balance begins in your heart, in your daily living. When you can go to bed each night and say I had a great day. I enjoyed my day. I had fun today!

When you are going to bed at night and say, I made it through another day. I survived another one. That does not sound or feel happy or content. It is time to do some internal searching within your heart to find what would really satisfy your Being.

You are who you are and nobody else can decide for you. You must feel it within. The knowingness that only you can say that feels right for you. Be you own therapist and identify what you desire.

Life has a way of working out for the most part. When you desire something, somehow it just appears or the right person will show up in your path to guide you. The universe works for us, for our greater good always. Choices are always available to us if we look for them.

Be open minded enough to see what is around you. Evaluate if you are where you want to be, and be willing to make the changes necessary. The universe will always provide for you. When one door closes another will open. You choose the door you want to take. You are the creator of your destiny.

Your current life is the product of the choices you have made along the way. If you are happy, you have made choices that support happiness. If you are discontent, you have made choices to put you here also. Change your choices and change your life.

Life, Balance, Relationships, Choices; these are all based on the same principle in your heart. What feels good vs. what does not?

Begin to make choices by asking yourself if it feels good. Here is a simple analogy. Going to lunch, where to go, burgers, chicken or sushi? Which feels better, if none then choose differently. Myself, I choose burgers over chicken and no sushi. If any feel good, then they are all the right choice. Whichever you choose would be equally satisfying. So it is true with life choices. If you get a knot in your stomach when thinking about an option, then maybe that isn't right. On the brighter side, if your option makes you smile and feels inspiring or intriguing to you, this is probably a better choice.

Vibration awareness covers every aspect of life: the thought process, the mental healing process, physical healing, and situational healing. It literally covers the entire gamut. Frequency is the key.

Science is trying to identify frequency but do not realize the huge scale to be defined. We have identified frequencies for radio, phones, electronics, etc., but we have not been able to fully identify all of the frequencies for healing.

It seems as though, if the pharmaceuticals knew this, they would shut it down. It would be the end to medicine in their fashion. But there is so much to gain in learning the frequencies and how they heal.

Music has healing tones. Frequency is everywhere. It surrounds us continuously. How you respond to the frequencies determines your health and well-being of your life!!

Recognized Perfection

The universe controls the timing of everything. They know the plan as setup before you came here. They know the exact timing before it all happens. Even if you think you are changing something, you're not. It was part of the grand scheme of your life plan. In all things, is perfect timing.

Even for me sitting here in this chair, feeling what I feel, writing these words. It is all perfectly in sync with the universe. The messages given by Doreen or Esther/Abraham. All are the influences planned for my growth and others. It's the timing of when I was exposed to it. The influences along the way. The validity of those on this path, and especially the Angels. I wish we could all see the many Angels that support us daily. I believe that would change the world.

Result of Vibration Awareness

Experiences that are pleasing to you will come as you eliminate the lower vibrations that are in your life. Be willing to experience the greatness the universe has to offer you.

Go with the flow and start acknowledging how you feel. This is the first step to understanding Vibration Awareness. I have already given you the chart. Now use it to acknowledge where you are on the chart. How do you feel? Recognizing your feelings, is feeling the vibration within. This is a great tool for continuous improvement.

If you want greater health and wellness, recognize how you feel. Pretty simple but you see amazing results. The more you actively try to improve your surroundings, the more these improved surroundings will come to you. Health and wellness are just a side benefit of being in a good place.

This may be more challenging for some than others. You can take this at surface level or you can go deep within and do some major clearing of your thought processes, beliefs, choices, and future outlook. You can choose to apply this to work or home or both. Is your life like a rollercoaster ride? Why? Evaluate your surroundings and see where the lows are. Maybe your job is the rollercoaster. What can be done to start making some simple adjustments to see what happens? Extreme highs and lows constantly bouncing back and forth are hard on your body. Find some middle ground to gain consistency for your health and welfare.

For the time being, acknowledge everything around you. Start to see how things affect you. What items or people have a bad effect on you? Once you have a mental list, next step is to set a few small changes in motion. What are you able to change? Maybe less time near or with this person/item that is a low vibration. Stay consistent and see if the situation improves. When you determine the changes you can make that have a positive impact. Then move on to more substantial changes. Remember to start small so you do not feel overwhelmed making changes all around you. Pick the worst case and make a small effort to lessen that in your life. When you feel the success of it, move on to the next object of disheartening feelings. Make those changes and keep going as needed.

Eventually you will find a place in your heart that says, I am finally at peace with everything around me and I feel good.

I will warn you, not all changes are going to be easy. There may need to be some uncomfortable conversations that need to take place to truly move forward. Whether with a coworker, a boss, a friend, or a family member, have the conversation from your HEART. You are speaking the truth of how you feel with love. It opens the door to healing and forgiveness necessary to move forward to a better space.

Wanting to be in a better place is nothing to be ashamed of. Admitting our lives are not perfect is okay too. We have all made choices at one time or another that we are not proud of, but nothing holds us in that space. We can make a new choice for a better place and go for it. We are allowed to have what makes us happy and content as long as it does not intentionally harm another.

You know, when we think of consequences, we think something bad. Like if I break the law, I need to pay the consequence for it, speeding = ticket. Well life is quite the same in a good way. You make a positive choice and then reap the consequence of a better living/working space. We usually call this "reap what you sow". Life can be great if you will allow it to come to you.

Vibration awareness in the workplace is a tough one. It is a belief that not all are going to take hold of. For management to grasp the reality of it will be the key to implementation. Work flow enhancers and other criteria to show how it works and functions. Then management will realize they do it already, follow the energy flow, they just didn't know it. It has never been identified in this context to them. Some do it naturally while others resist. Those that resist, are resistant to any change or movement outside of their routine. It takes time for these individuals to come around.

Today is yesterday's tomorrow. Keep at it.

Awareness of Change

A joyful or joy filled life is in how your body interprets it. Laughter is great. Smirks are great too. It is an acknowledgement to your body that you are on the right path. You are getting amusement out of something.

My intent in writing this book is to awaken your DNA's awareness. To activate you, to wake up your spirit/heart, to connect to source to realize we are all of the same maker but with different talents. Does not mean one is greater than another but does mean we work better as one connected.

Being aware of frequency, the law of attraction, is a way of acknowledging a better, calmer way of life for things to flow smoothly. Yes this is true to all. Reap what you sow.

Everyone can tap into their energy source and use it to heal themselves. They can open their heart to greater possibilities.

Time Awareness

As I mentioned before, time is an illusion yet we use it as a foundation of living. Where has the time gone? What happened to it, who configured it? Why do we feel we need it? Is it because we are so discontent with who we are or what we do, that we can't wait for the time to be over? Like a prison sentence here with all the rules and regulations, boundaries all about us. When our heart just wants to be free from the bondage of time. Free to be, to explore, to love.

These are our truest challenges to living and being. Conquer love, conquer time, conquer confinement, and yet allow ourselves to be free in our heart. So how do we do this?

We open our awareness of our heart within. We allow ourselves to love and be loved. We accept the journey of here and now to move beyond. We love unconditionally to open the doors within that releases the boundaries of time and space. We expand our passion for life and share it with others. This is the total fulfillment of all that is.

Magnificence of the Universe

ᔪᔭ

Have you ever just marveled at the universe? Seen the magnificence in it? The colors? The beautiful colors of the flowers, the blooms. They are like humans or actually humans are like the flowers. We all bloom at different times. We are like the trees that they have different species as do we have different races. Yet in the end we all serve a purpose.

Have you ever really looked at the sky? Have you thought about it? Each day is a new picture. Each minute is different as the clouds move. The sky is never the same. It's beautiful. The morning sunrise colors and the evening sunsets. Each one is uniquely different. As are we. We are all beautiful, wear our own colors, yet uniquely different but the same.

We have a grand creator. Look at the beauty and magnificence around us. Each day is a new scene. A new page in our story and the universe story. We are all one, connected by this source that cares for us so deeply. Gives us beautiful pictures of nature every day. Shares his splendor with us at no cost. Just to show his love for us.

Be thankful each day. Each moment you see the beauty and know that you are part of the beauty. Our creator has dressed us as well. Look around you and take mental pictures. See the beauty in your kitchen, out a window, at a bedspread, your parents, a child, a husband, a clock, a plate, a piece of furniture, your neighbor. Beauty surrounds us if we look for it!

Afterword: Applying principles to your work/life

Applying to your Work and Life

Time and consequences. What does it have to do with vibration awareness? Everything!! All things meant to be will happen in their due time. The consequences of the actions taken are dependent on the timing of it. If you are not in sync with the timing of implementing something, then the consequence is not getting the desired outcome. On the other hand, if you wait on the correct timing to take action, then you could reap the rewards of the implementation as expected.

Now begs the question: how do you know if the timing is right or not? Right? The answer to the question is the filling in the pie. The key to life.

If everything in your life happened exactly as you planned, you would not be asking this question in the first place would you.

We have all experienced circumstances in life and work that did not go as planned. Then we have often wondered why not. All of the pieces were there, you put in place but for some unknown reason things went awry.

Timing was your factor that you did not consider or maybe you did. It was specific to an implementation plan, had to be pushed because of budget or other circumstances. Where did that get you? All it did was set you back on time right? Now you are late getting it going or it is too late to begin or too late period!!

What value did you place on time? Yes this is a real question. What value did you place on time? Was it in the budget for a specific quarter or year? Was it because the product had a deadline and why pay for something if you're not going to get it implemented? Most corporate scenarios time sequence revolves around money, quarters, write-offs, stakeholders, mitigation, audit, and/or continuous improvement plans for shareholders.

Timing is a free agent and does not revolve around any of these items. Timing revolves around energy. Energy of the project/application/experience to be implemented.

What does that energy feel like? Yes another one of these questions. What does the ENERGY FEEL like? It's not about the expected outcome or who or what is pushing something to be implemented. It is about how it feels. Does it truly feel right in your heart? Deep down do you feel it, do you really feel it is absolutely the best scenario or product or project to engage in at this immediate time? Leave the business out of it for a while. Make a list of pros and cons from your heart and truly feel the response.

In the universe, there is this law of attraction. What you put out, you get back. In other words, reap what you sow. Like energy attracts like energy whether you believe in it or not. Your heart is true energy at the core. So if you can put the pros and cons up on a board and weigh the energy of each, you can come up with a reasonable outcome one way or the other.

How do you weigh the energy? When you think of each item, whether good or bad, how does it make you feel? On a scale of 1 to 10, 10 feeling the best and 1 not pleased and need a different option, never going to really work and you know in your heart it is a waste of time and energy. Then the highest score wins.

But does it, how bad do you want to implement no matter what the consequences? If you took the higher score assuming the pros side won, it may look something like this:

Pros

1. Product need = 8
2. Ease of use = 8
3. End value = 8
4. Training offered = 10
5. Support = 10

Score = 44

Cons

1. Product expense = 3
2. Effort to use = 3
3. Amount of involvement required = 4
4. Labor expense to rollout = 4
5. Training expense = 6
6. Expertise required = 9
7. Warranty/support = 7

Score = 36

So if I took pros 44 – cons 36 = 8 overall energy commit rating looks good. It's above 5 by a fair margin and seems to be a valid move forward number.

Now I'm going to change the cons slightly to look at this from another angle.

<u>Cons</u>

1. Product expense = 3
2. Effort to use = 3
3. Amount of involvement required = 4
4. Labor expense to rollout = 8
5. Training expense = 6
6. Expertise required = 9
7. Warranty/support = 7

Score = 40

Now the pros score is still 44 – cons 40 = 4 for an overall energy commit. The number is less than half way so this may not be your best product. Yes the pros outweighed the cons but by a small margin. Enough to go back to the drawing board and look for another option or wait for something to shift the pros and cons to warrant another evaluation.

Of course if the cons totally outweighed the pros, then most definitely stop in your tracks. Let's play with the idea of the final number between the pros and cons being midway at 6 or 7. It is above the halfway point and could very well be a viable option. I would ask myself how I truly felt about it, pros and cons aside. How do you feel? If it still feels right then move forward.

This is just a sample of how to find the happy medium. In order for the scale to truly work, you must be honest with yourself and leave all the other variables for implementation out. You must feel it.

Each manager or department involved could solicit their teams to see what kind of scores each team returns. You could compare the scores to see how many reach the implementation mark or not. If not, you would want to know why.

I know they say do not take things to heart. Comments made, or actions of some, or attitudes, whatever the case may be, but by getting their input, shows you care. It shows your honest intentions are not driven by just "do this because you are told to", but it shows you are willing to listen and feel their energy input into a project.

Smaller companies tend to have better synergy with their employees than larger companies. Large companies tend to send directives down but never accept input from below. Smaller companies are more on level with their employees. Large companies become disconnected from the workers doing the actual work. It's really a matter of perspective if you choose to see it.

Creating synergy is creating energy. Which level of energy do you choose to create, one of reap what you sow, getting back what you gave out. So what does that look like? Is it on the top end of the scale where the majority feel good about it or is it a push either way because it has to be done in a specific time frame. What is the cost of something not working as expected and when do you call it quits or try with a different means? Time can be our friend. It'll either show us when we push too hard, yet stand still or it will flow endlessly with ease throughout. How do you want time to respond to you?

What do you push with little reward and what flows with ease and just works seamlessly? Take time to look back and take an inventory of past projects/products. Be honest with yourself. How many are still in use and useful? How many are not fully implemented? How many are not even recognized anymore? How overwhelmed or not are your people from taking on one project or product after another? Do you provide continuous training for each product for each employee, new or existing? Is it face to face training?

Face to face training can increase synergy of a product. Whereas computer based training videos that just tell about it and are not interaction in a human one on one sort of way, take energy away from a process.

Creating live energy and feeling it are the core of making life work whether it is on the job or off. Your heart drives you, each choice. Wouldn't you rather be pleased with the choices you make? Feeling the good that is accomplished.

How often do you walk away from work and feel drained? Did it suck the life out of you? Or did you walk away with a sense of accomplishment? How do you feel? Did you make choices today that where pushed on you or that you agreed with and felt good about?

At home, are you happy to get home each day or not? What is waiting for you? Have you made choices of a happy home? Family? Or are you strict and do not allow fun in. Are you serious about life or do you laugh?

Yes laughter is actually the best medicine. Learn to laugh and have laughter around you. It is a high energy of wellbeing and good health. Your work environment should consist of some light hearted atmosphere to promote health and wellbeing. The healthy employees take less or no sick days. Less sick days helps the company's bottom line.

Creating a live and synergetic environment is key to success in any form.

Unhappy employees breed more unhappy employees. Like attracts like. Unhappy employees are typically stressed due to workload, or doing a job that they are not fit for. Lots of companies do re-orgs for whatever reason and do not take into account the value of a person doing something they like vs. shifting them to another role.

Stirring the pot is not always a good thing. Look at skillset. Yes they may have the talent or ability but do they want to? This "want to" can make or break a company. They can lose many great employees by not listening to them. Either they leave due to discontent, or they do not apply their talent because they don't like it, or not comfortable with it. Some will ride the gravy train for as long as they can doing little as possible until discharged or retired.

What type of workforce do you want working for you? And bigger question, do you even know your workforce? Really know them?

Do you hear laughter, do you see smiles, and do you hear pleasant hellos? Or do you hear idle chit chat of discontent? Are managers dealing with struggles continuously? It doesn't have to be hard, letting your managers manage in a way that empowers synergy between employees can solve its own issues. Putting people in places that they have interest is key.

I say this, but you may be thinking well yeah they applied for that job. But what you don't see are the department re-orgs that have taken place over time and the person is no longer where they were hired to be. They were moved to fill a need.

Paying attention to your surroundings is important. You can learn a lot about people, places and things if you hang around long enough to experience the truth of the environment.

What stands out? What speaks to you? Does anything in the environment intrigue you?

Is it dull or boring? Is it lively but stable? Is it clean and fits the needs or old and antiquated? The environment is an energy also. Not one to be taken lightly. It must be fitting and conducive to working yet free enough to be flexible.

Reducing timelines and deadlines while creating an environment of flexibility actually produces more from employees. Giving freedom to work on their own terms to a certain degree goes a long way to reducing sick time and unpaid time off.

Happy is healthy!

As we stated before, time and space have their own continuum. Time and space are an illusion to a certain degree. Earth is full of time and less space. The atmosphere above is more space and less time. The balance in life is about putting these two together in a fashion that is beneficial to your life, to your goals. It's about the balance restored to receive more with less. Yes less. Less struggle, less fight, less friction, to gain more with ease.

The goal in life is to get what we want and be successful. Right? And have some abundance of cash along the way to enhance the joys available in life, vacations, extras, etc.

So let's enjoy the ability to get more with less. Awareness is the first step. You must first be aware of your stress, your struggles, and the friction that may surround you.

Secondly, you must believe in an effortless way of doing business. If you are constantly pushing to make something happen then the timing is not right. All should flow with ease. What is blocking you? Step back and be the observer. Is it a person or business plan that is holding back your success? Is it your thought process?

Are you grateful for where you are? Are you grateful for the things that are working as well as those that appear to block you? What could you learn from the block? When you figure that out and are thankful for the block enhancing your learning, you may move forward once again.

Ask for guidance or help along the way. There are many sources and resources of guidance to help smooth out any troubles you may be having. Asking for help is part of the process. Being thankful for the help is even bigger. People, places, and things seem to move and change continuously. Are you able to float? Yes float. That means coast on the wave when necessary. Slow down till the riptide is through and then continue on. While you are floating, take it all in and see what you can learn. What can you learn from the events, changes that have temporarily paused your status in time?

Think about the events and how they affect your bottom line. Now what do you need to change to keep moving along and not be outdated, but to keep up to speed. It will flow flawlessly if you go with the tides of time.

In all things there is a season and then change as seasons do. Be mindful of the normal ups and downs and then they will not get you down. Prepare your mind in advance for change along the way. Simple modifications go a long way towards a fruitful end.

Epilogue

Age is all about how a person perceives their life. The young at heart will potentially live longer because they have a desire to keep moving. This all comes back to your heart. Your heart really is the center of all things spiritual and earthly. It truly is about following your heart.

Feeling overwhelmed because you don't seem to know how your heart feels? Daylight, warmth feel good and energize you. Why? This is what your heart wants. Sitting at work behind closed doors, at a desk, tied to your computer screen, feels draining. Why? Because your heart does not want that. It used to feel good to do hands on in the datacenter, now not so much.

Keep moving to find what energizes you. I actually like to be outdoors, dogs, horses, cows, farm life. These feel good, feel natural to me. I like to share profound insights I am given, to those willing to listen. It's important for everyone to find their niche and expand on it. Finding something that speaks to you and your heart are life lessons that surpass time and space.

Do not fear others. Fear is opposite of truth. Fear is illusion. Truth is real. Always search for the truth. Look within to find the greatest truth of ever, reveal who you are.

I move forward in knowingness of the universe plan of life. Of life to be and life to come. I move forward in action to complete a process. A process of being, living, and loving. I am the love of God and am here to share that. I am to share the life that God wants for all of us. I am to present it in this book.

I am loved and led by God and the Angels above and beyond. They light my path and guide my way. They keep me moving in the right direction. I am so blessed to have such guidance and support from the realm beyond reality. From beyond the seen and can only be felt in the deepest sense of our spirits. I can help open that up in you if you so choose. It's available to all who ask. Thank you.

Knowing what I know, being spirit in human form. This is what we are here to learn. We are eternal and this earthliness is temporary. We are to live in love of each other and all things.

So what do I do now? What's left here? To teach others, show them how to get to this place. Show love to your family and all around you. Just SHARE LOVE!! That's it. Now let life flow. You can have or do any job you want. It's not about the job or career choice. It's about the love you share while you do it. Sharing love travels to all. That is the key.

Word from the Wise:

Go about your business today and just flat out be nice always. Don't take anything personal. Do the best you can always. That's it, simple. Life will be rewarded as you learn to love unconditionally.

In all things be Thankful:

Thank you for the instruction on living life. Learning to love unconditionally fulfills the spirit for eternity. Thank you. I appreciate all you do for me, the inspiration and love. Thank you so much! Thank you for finding the shards of my past and putting them back together. Thank you for the healing within and beyond. Thank you for the alignment of my being. Thank you for making me whole again. Life is wonderful. I am blessed with my Angels and God, Universe and Guides, all my spirit realm support. I could not do it without you. You are wonderful. Thank you. I feel I can't say thank you enough. That there is no earthly word that expresses it strong enough. I am so grateful!!

The Future Continues – More to come

And so my journey continues. Doors open and resources are made available. All part of the divine plan. I am so excited to share my journey, my discoveries, the healing, the angels, and the universe energy. So many things to share with so many.

I am excited to share the start of it all and the road I have travelled. The doubts, the possibilities, the learning, the acceptance, that feeling of finally knowing what is right for me. Just that feeling of knowing how perfect the universe is and nothing is by chance. You are exactly where you are meant to be at every moment. The feeling when you know everything is right with the world and the people around me. My choices are always right on target and my path is increasing in credibility every moment. The flow of the universe to me, the encouragement of the angels, and the abundance that continues to flow in. The realization of how amazing this life can be and that we are eternal all the same.

I am excited to share my past life discoveries. The format of how that all developed and transpired. Realizing I could or that I was channeling angels and the journaling adventure. The powerful messages I received on so many topics and the internal healing I received throughout it all.

To learn and know why certain things resonate with me. Like the uneasiness of flying only to find out later about Amelia. Then how strongly the energy stuff resonated with me only to learn about Krishna years later. The love of nature, Indian jewelry, animals, trees, bear, wolf, and elephant. The relation to dreams I had. Everybody has their thing. It will be exposed to them when the time is right.

People may think I am strange to believe in this. But the fact is, it exists whether you believe or not. So why not try to learn and understand. It makes things much easier and life progression flows much more smoothly knowing who is truly in control.

The younger you learn about being an eternal being and love is the key, the less garbage you need to deal with, heal and confront. You can move forward with the true journey to help humanity "live in love – abide in love".

It comes back to helping people care about people. Be nice to one another. Respect each other!

Acknowledgements

I would like to thank the Universe for providing the material to me. For reaching deep inside to reveal from within my experiences and relating then to the here and now for a greater tomorrow. Today is yesterday's tomorrow!!

I would like to thank my husband Doug for sticking with me and seeing this through. He had doubts along the way but we made it so far.

I want to thank my daughters (Tabi and Kelli), and the rest of my family for the life experiences. Good and bad, for the lessons learned and more to come. Thank you Kelli for being my rock!

Thanks to my friends at work and home. You know who you are. For the inspiration to keep plugging away to get this done so you don't have to hear about it anymore. You have been part of my rollercoaster ride. Thanks for enduring ME!

A special thanks to Chris Villani for the hypnosis sessions that helped reveal a deeper perspective of what this is truly about underneath it all. What an experience!!

And to my Energy Guru Candene without whom none of this would have ever begun. It's been quite a journey and it's not over yet. Not even close!!

Inspiration for the book to come to life

თადედ

True blue I feel.
The respect of others
Flows on, blue to blue.
Love is real, love is fine,
Time to be genuine.
Feel the blast, work within,
Time will tell the groove you're in.
You are a candle on a dark summer day,
Your light shines keenly to those below;
Watch your back, for time is gone,
Nowhere to hide, only ties that bind.
You are strong, you are weak, you are loves defeat.
Take time for pleasure, time for pain,
The wrath is upon you, with much to gain.
Ride the wave, enjoy the waters,
Blue today, Blue tomorrow.
BLUE

Excerpts of
Future Books

Awareness of Time/ Memories - Discovering DNA, What is it? What does it mean for you?

Our lives come and go yet our souls continue on. They are eternal you know. The powerful soul can return to remember places and times, people and things, events that we should have lost in the passing but didn't. So here we are seeing them in dreams, in portals of time just an arm's length away.

What do we do with these memories? Savor them. For what you say? What have they got to do with here and now? They have shaped you, your heart, and your soul. They are the beliefs that shape you into who and what you are today. Revel in it, see where they take you. What do you wish to let go of or keep? Are they true or truth? How does that make you feel? Each life builds on another. Keep the good stuff and let go of the bad. Let go of what does not hold truth for you today!

Be fair to yourself. Know all is for good at the time. Recount your lessons learned, now you can keep the lesson learned and release the so called bad.

Recount your blessings with care and love. You are strong and all is for good, for learning.

Our life lessons not only affect us from one lifetime to another, but also each generation on down the line. The beliefs we live by are passed on to our children. Whichever of those beliefs they choose to live by, get carried on again and so the system goes.

Our souls take those beliefs and lessons with it into the spirit realm and back again, but not necessarily into the same family generational tree. Rather within our souls, for whomever we become. So tracking our DNA, our past is not as true as you may think. There is physical DNA as the generational tree and then the spirit DNA of who we have been. Past life regression can tell us who we have been from a spirit soul point of view. From there its meditation, dreams, and energy healing that recover who you are at the depths of your soul. Like peeling back the layers of an onion or lotus flower.

Who do you want to know? Your choice!!

Recognizing Diverse Lives – Where will the next life lead?

⚬⚬⚬

Ready to roll, stories from the past. Which past right? The here and now or our spiritual past. What is truth? What is living? How do we define life?

Stories unfold as we live. The people and circumstances in your life all have a bearing of who you are. They tell the stories of your past. Your likes and dislikes underneath it all, it tells a story. The story of your life experiences from a past beyond and you relive it today.

Getting to the root of our story is part of the journey. The journey to find out who you really are. The lessons you have learned and those you have not. So many of us question, who am I, what am I doing here. Deep down they know there is more than meets the eye.

What do you think your past looks like? Who was in it then vs. who is in it now? How does knowing this change who we are or who we thought we were? What influence from our past is affecting us now? Is it a lesson we refuse to learn? Was it a horrible death and you are afraid of death now? Was it a forbidden love and what bearing does that have on you now? So many questions and yet seemingly so few answers.

Are you drawn to medieval times? Was that significant in your past? Are you drawn to mafia movies or certain characters? Could this have been you in the past? Why does it still affect you? What are you supposed to learn? What is the significant event?

Once we identify some of these characteristics that keep coming into our lives. We can ask for the reason to be revealed to us. Sit and meditate for a few minutes. Ask in earnest devotion for more to be revealed to you. Maybe it was a way of living that you are to rectify. A lesson in how you treated others and needs to be remedied at the root of your being.

So many scenarios and each will be slightly different. How many times have you come back to learn the same lessons? Why do you struggle with learning? What could be done to help you move forward?

My lives have been revealed to me in some strange ways. At first all I knew was that I was on my eleventh life here. Then I started asking in meditation for them to be revealed to me. I went to a fair called "The Shift Charlotte". A form of psychic fair I suppose you could say. A lot of healers and readers, those who believe in the spirit realm. I was drawn to this art. Endura Art where you could see faces in the background of pictures. It intrigued me, so I signed up for a class.

While in the class we were asked to pick a picture. Look into the eyes of the person in the picture and channel their energy. I had no idea who I had chosen. I never channeled anyone's energy either. I just honestly looked at the picture and the woman's face. Then we closed our eyes and drew our Endura art picture. Then the instructor came around to tell us about it. She said my colors I chose meant death (red) and then some other stuff. She also told me I had chosen Krishna, a male by the way that looked like a woman in the picture to me. She said the red and brown represented his death, then proceeded to tell me how he died. I did not feel that death at all, the way she explained it. It felt much harsher to me.

Shortly after all this, I happen to read a book, Many Lives, Many Masters by Brian Weiss. That is when it all began to fall into place for me. The identities, one by one, were revealed to me. One of them being Krishna, which explains why I did not feel the death she told me was true. I felt it differently because it was me and was in my subconscious, inner being.

Sometimes we just need to follow our heart and let it lead us. The answers will come when we are ready. As life passes by, more is revealed in the universe timeline. Each phase has its moments and its perfect timing. When we are ready to accept the truth of eternal life, unending spirit, that returns to learn and grow, the universe will reveal it to us. Life everlasting as the Catholic priests say during mass.

Printed in the United States
By Bookmasters